SWIFT

© Copyright 2019 by _____MG Martin___ - All rights reserved.

The following Book is reproduced below with the goal of providing information that is as accurate and reliable as possible. Regardless, purchasing this eBook can be seen as consent to the fact that both the publisher and the author of this book are in no way experts on the topics discussed within and that any recommendations or suggestions that are made herein are for entertainment purposes only. Professionals should be consulted as needed prior to undertaking any of the actions endorsed herein.

This declaration is deemed fair and valid by both the American Bar Association and the Committee of Publishers Association and is legally binding throughout the United States.

Furthermore, the transmission, duplication, or reproduction of any of the following work including specific information will be considered an illegal act irrespective of whether it is done electronically or in print. This extends to creating a secondary or tertiary copy of the work or a recorded copy and is only allowed with the express written consent from the Publisher. All additional rights reserved.

The information in the following pages is broadly considered to be a truthful and accurate account of facts, and as such any inattention, use or misuse of the information in question by the reader will render any resulting actions solely under their purview. There are no scenarios in which the publisher or the original author of this work can be, in any fashion, deemed liable for any hardship or damages that may befall them after undertaking information described herein.

Additionally, the information in the following pages is intended only for informational purposes and should thus be thought of as universal. As befitting its nature, it is presented without assurance regarding its prolonged validity or interim quality. Trademarks are mentioned without written consent and can in no way be considered an endorsement from the trademark holder.

TABLE OF CONTENTS

SWIFT
Basic Fundamental Guide for Beginners

Introduction 3

Chapter 1: Introduction To Swift Programming 4

    Set up your mac 5

    First, Sign Up As A Developer: 5

    Have Your Credentials Ready: 6

    Choose Your Program: 6

    Getting Ready Your Environment: 6

    The Source Control: 7

Chapter 2: Working With Collections In Swift 8

    The "Mutability" Of The Collections: 9

    Arrays: 9

    Array Type: 9

    Empty Array in Swift: 10

    Array Which Have A Default Value 10

    How To Create An Array By Combining Two Arrays: 11

    Using The Array Literal To Create An Array: 11

    Access And Modify An Array: 12

    Iterate Over An Array: 15

    Sets: 16

    Hash Values - Set Types: 17

The Set Type Syntax: 17

Creating And Initializing Empty Set 18

Creating A Set Using Array Literal: 18

Chapter 3: Control Statements And Decisions In Loops 20

Loops: 20

The For Loop In Swift: 21

We Start With The For-In Loops: 22

Now, Let's Turn Our Attention To
The For-Condition-Increment Loops 26

Swift While Loops: 28

Conditions In Swift 29

The If Statements 29

Switch Statements: 30

Transferring Control: 31

Chapter 4: Swift Functions 32

Writing Functions in Swift Language: 32

Not Just Numbers Alone: 35

Paremeters AD NAUSEAM 37

First Class Functions: 39

"Throw me a function" 41

Function In A Function: 44

Default Parameters: 47

What is contained in the name? 49

Chapter 5: Structures and Classes in Swift 52

Classes, Structures, and Enumerations: 52

Class Declaration: 54

Import Declarations: 57

Declaring A Class: 57

Subclass Declaration: 57

Base Class Declaration: 58

Using A Protocol: 58

How To Declare A Subclass And Use A Protocol? 58

Base Class And Protocol: 58

Declaration Of The Structure: 59

Declaring enum: 59

Components and Subcomponents: 60

The Body: 61

The UI Actions And The Outlets For Classes Alone: 61

Chapter 6: Making Better Swift Apps 62

Tips: 62

Enhance The Readability Of The Constants: 62

Keep away from "NSObject and @objc"
to enhance the performance 63

Make Use Of The Swizzling Method In Swift 63

Tips For New Beginners In Swift 64

You Should Make It A Practice To Clean Up Your
Asynchronous Code: 64

Regulate The Access To The Code: 65

Make Use Of The Optional In The Right Manner:........................ 65

The NSNumber should be left behind: 66

Tips On How You Should Not Develop Apps In IOS: 66

Conclusion 69

SWIFT
A Comprehensive Intermediate Guide to Learn and Master the Concept of Swift Programming

Introduction 73

Chapter 1: Building Adaptive User Interface.................................75
Size Classes... 76

Chapter 2: Add Section and Index List in the UITableView............81
Demo App 82

How to display Sections in the UITableView 83

Chapter 3: Creating Simple View Animations in Swift....................86
The Basic View Animations 87

Spring Animations 88

Keyframe Animations.. 89

View Transitions.. 89

Chapter 4: JSON and Codable 91
Importance of Coding and Decoding 91

The Codable Protocol.. 93

Decode with JSON Codable... 95

Encode Objects with JSON Codable... 97

Chapter 5: Get Social with Swift 99

The initial Setup 100

Import Framework 100

Interface Design 100

Add Facebook Support 102

Point to note 102

Twitter Support 102

Add image to the post 104

Chapter 6: Send SMS AND MMS in Swift language 106

A demo app 106

Let's get started 106

Import Message UI Framework 107

How to implement the Delegate? 107

Creating the Message Composer 108

Time to compile and run the app 109

Suppose you don't prefer in-app SMS 109

Chapter 7: Custom Fonts and Dynamic Type 111

The Dynamic Type 111

Scale A Custom Font 113

Font Metrics 113

Style Dictionary 114

Custom Font 116

Override the iOS Dynamic Type font family 118

Modify Font Descriptors 118

The global font family overrides appearance proxy 119

Chapter 8: Create Better iOS Animations 121

The importance of Interactive Animations 121

UIViewProprtyAnimator 122

A popup Menu 124

Chapter 9: Create a today widget in Swift Language 132

Definition of an extension 132

The Today extension 133

The Target Setup 133

Chapter 10: UICollectionView Custom Layout 136

Create a custom collection view layout 136

Core Layout Process 138

How can you calculate the attributes? 139

Chapter 11: Get Directions and Draw routes in Swift 146

Directions and Draw routes in Swift 146

Conclusion 148

SWIFT
Advanced Detailed Approach To
Master Swift Programming with Latest Updates

Introduction 151

Chapter 1: Swift Latest Updates 152

How is the Swift 5.0 Update implemented? 153

The Purpose of Swift 5.0: ABI Stability 155

The ABI Stability Manifesto 155

What is ABI? 156

Requirements of ABI Stability... 156

Integer Multiples using "isMultiple(of:)" 159

The result type... 161

Dealing with Future Enum Cases... 162

Flatten Nested Options with "try?"... 165

Chapter 2: Variable Types and Constants 168

Integers.. 168

Integer bounds 168

Int.. 168

Variables and Constants in Swift... 169

Swift variables and constant type 171

Inferring types using Type Inference.. 173

Chapter 3: Value Types vs Reference Types 174

The Value Types in Swift.. 174

Value Types in Swift 175

Reference Types in Swift 177

The Value types vs reference types 179

Mutability using "let" And "var" 179

Practical IOS Development 180

Using APIs 181

Creating your own APIs and types 181

Determine the equality or identicality.. 181

Independent state.. 182

Any Object in Swift.. 182

Why implement any and any object?.. 184

The difference between *Any* and *AnyObject*. 185

Chapter 4: Swift Functions and For Loop 188

How to define and Call functions... 188

Function arguments and parameters 191

The Function Return Types and Values 193

Generics in Swift Explained... 194

Chapter 5: Map, Reduce and Filter in Swift 205

Applying the Map Function... 207

Using the Reduce Function 209

Conclusion 211

SWIFT

Basic Fundamental Guide for Beginners

Introduction

Congratulations on purchasing *SWIFT :Basic Fundamental Guide For Beginners* and thank you for doing so.

There are plenty of books on this subject on the market, thanks again for choosing this one! Every effort was made to ensure it is full of as much useful information as possible, please enjoy!

Swift is among the new languages which you can use to code for OS X apps as well as the IOS apps. The language for technology is to learn to code, and there is no better way to take your coding skills than learning to code using Swift language. You will learn how you can solve real-world problems at a go as well as work in a creative manner. Swift language will help you build apps which every apple user would want to use. With Swift language, you have the ability to create something which can change the world.

Still a new language, Swift provides a change for the macOS and apple developers. Experienced apple developers will have something new to learn while the new developers have a chance to learn Swift language. Swift language is one of the best languages for every iOS and macOS developer. Every new language has a lot of things to learn. And that is also true with the Swift language.

In this book, we shall help you experience the fun of coding with Swift language. Writing code can sometimes be tiresome, it can also be intriguing. There is something lovely and enjoyable while writing a line of code, not forgetting the greatest joy that one feels after creating an app which solves a problem in the world. It is said, the best way to become a professional developer is to practice to code. If that is the case, we can get started! In case you start to feel like this is not for you, don't give up. Keep reading and I am sure you may surprise yourself.

Chapter 1

Introduction To Swift Programming

Swift is the new language to use to develop in apps in Apple. The language is applied in OS X and IOS devices. Swift replaces Apple's IOS and OS X languages. The greatest thing with Swift is that it has been designed to work well with the Objective-C.

There are a few beginners to Swift programming who start to learn the language with some expertise in other languages such as C, Objective - C and the C++.

Regardless of your level of experience, Swift is the right language to get started. In this chapter, we shall help you kick the ball rolling.

Some of the important devices which you will need to have to run your Swift programs include:

- Mac Laptop or computer. If you have the latest Mac, you will be good to go because it has sufficient memory and processor speed.

- The XCode. This is the IDE for building iOS apps and the OS X apps. You can get it for free if you visit the App store for Mac.

These are some of the important things which you need to have. They are enough to help you begin coding in Swift. However, if you can still add some additional tools, it can be very beneficial on your side. Still, if you don't have the extra tools, no need to worry. They include:

- A device of the iOS if you are going to work on the iOS platform. While you can still go ahead and develop an apple app without having a testing device, you will be shocked by the results when you begin to see some of the reviews written by people. Just developing an apple app by following what is written in blog posts is something difficult. I will suggest you look for a real apple device. With an Apple device, things become easier. Unless you plan to develop something which does not need a user interface. This could be a large component of a given app.

- Internet access. Don't worry if you don't have a strong internet access. You can still develop even though you will experience some limitations. There are a few operations including uploading your app into the app store which will need you to have an internet connection.

- Sufficient disk space. Sufficient disk space means your internal disk or even external disk connected to your Mac. You need to ensure you have a backup alternative for all your projects.

Apple has a discussion forum the same way Android developers have a forum. I will suggest that you join the Apple forums to be able to associate and communicate with fellow developers.

Set up your mac

Here we help you learn how you can prepare your Mac ready to develop in Swift. We provide you with the basic steps.

First, Sign Up As A Developer:

The basic tools of a developer are free; this means you can begin to learn Swift programming immediately. However, Apple needs you to sign up as a developer on their developer website before you get the chance to use many of their developer tools and features. Some of the features you need don't require registration. There are crucial features which will need you to register, especially, when it comes to testing your App.

Besides the registration, there is a point where you will have to sign the non-disclosure agreement. Here, you will receive an invitation to participate in a developer program which you might have to pay some fee. However, if you aren't stable financially or perhaps you have a limited budget, you can opt not to join the program. Something which you should note is that the guidelines for developing apps in Apple change with time. It is also different from one country to another. Always go back to the developer website to familiarize yourself with the latest information and rules.

Have Your Credentials Ready:

To sign up with Apple, you have to provide your Apple ID. Remember that your Apple ID is not private. Only the password is confidential. You can have more than one Apple IDs. In certain cases, you will find developers who have an additional Apple ID for their own use.

Choose Your Program:

Apple has several developer programs for you to register. The easiest program is the individual program which now costs about $99 per year, as well as a separate program for the OS X and IOS. If you decide to enroll for the two, you will have to pay about $198.

Still, you can enroll as a business entity. This will help you to come up with teams made up of individual developers. At the same time, you can share the code among your developers. Also, it has programs for educational institutions. But, make sure you have an Apple ID to use it for your development.

Getting Ready Your Environment:

The environment you are going to use to develop your Swift program will be the XCode and the Mac. Ensure that you have installed the XCode. XCode is provided freely, and it is easy to install. If you have access to a computer lab at school, XCode could be a component already at the lab.

There are no complicated settings to use XCode with Swift language. All you need to do is to select Swift language instead of the objective C in the pop-up menu which comes up. You will need to further get the latest Swift documentation and SDK. However, this is part of the basic installation process.

The Source Control:

The source control comes in-built with the XCode alongside the Git and Subversion. As a result of its architecture, Git has been closely combined with XCode compared to Subversion. Using any of these tools helps you store your code in the repository. Make it a practice to store your code in the repository so that you can download your source code at any time.

A source control allows you to use your source code at any time and any place, as long as you have a mac computer and internet connection.

Chapter 2

Working With Collections In Swift

Swift language has three types of collection. They include the arrays, sets and the dictionaries. All these collection types help one store values. Arrays consist of a collection of ordered items. The sets comprise of unordered collections of special values while the dictionaries comprise of unordered collections of "key-value associations".

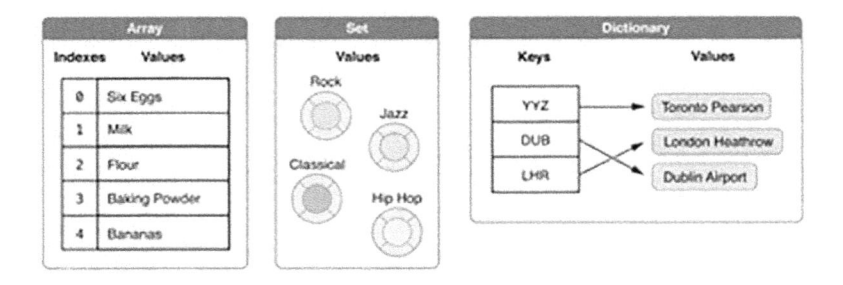

Array			Set	Dictionary	
Indexes	Values		Values	Keys	Values
0	Six Eggs		Rock	YYZ	Toronto Pearson
1	Milk		Jazz	DUB	London Heathrow
2	Flour		Classical	LHR	Dublin Airport
3	Baking Powder		Hip Hop		
4	Bananas				

All the above three types of collections are clear concerning the kinds of values which they can store as well as the keys. What this means is that it is difficult for one to insert a wrong type of value into a given collection by mistake.

Furthermore, you can still be sure about the type of values which you want to extract from a given collection.

Note:

We implement dictionary, sets and arrays in Swift language as a generic collection.

The "Mutability" Of The Collections:

Well, if you decide to create a dictionary, array or set and then allocate it a variable, we consider the created collection to be mutable. We say it is mutable because you have the ability to modify the collection once it is created. You can do this by either subtracting, adding or even perform some modification of the items inside. If you opt to allocate a set, dictionary or array to a constant, the collection becomes "**immutable**". Thus, we can't change the size and contents.

Note:

It is a nice practice to have immutable collections in almost all situations especially when the collection is not supposed to be modified. By doing this way, it makes everything easy for one to read and understand the code. Furthermore, a compiler in Swift will help improve the level of performance of the collection.

Arrays:

Arrays hold values of related items in an ordered list. The values can still appear in the array many times at various positions.

Note:

The Swift's array type has been bridged to the Foundation's NSArray class.

Array Type:

We write the Swift array in full like **Array<Element>,** in this case, the Element refers to the type of values found in the array. It is possible to write the array type in a different way which is fast and short [Element]. Even though both forms are similar, most developers prefer to use the second method because of how easy it is.

Empty Array in Swift:

In Swift language, the initializer syntax allows one to create an empty array:

```
1  var someInts = [Int]()
2  print("someInts is of type [Int] with \(someInts.count) items.")
3  // Prints "someInts is of type [Int] with 0 items."
```

You should pay attention here and see that the **someInts** variable has been referred to **[Int] right from the type** of initializer.

At the same time, if we have the context already with the type of information such as typed constant or variable, it is possible to go ahead and build an empty array which has literal, this can be written with the []:

```
1  someInts.append(3)
2  // someInts now contains 1 value of type Int
3  someInts = []
4  // someInts is now an empty array, but is still of type [Int]
```

Array Which Have A Default Value.

When dealing with arrays in Swift, it offers one the ability to create an array of a certain size which will hold the default values. You do this by setting the initializer with a default value of the correct type. This is called **repeating.** The number of times the value appears in the array is referred to as **count**:

```
1  var threeDoubles = Array(repeating: 0.0, count: 3)
2  // threeDoubles is of type [Double], and equals [0.0, 0.0, 0.0]
```

How To Create An Array By Combining Two Arrays:

In Swift language, it is possible to have a new array by just integrating two existing arrays by using the addition symbol. The only thing to consider is that the arrays should be compatible.

```
1   var anotherThreeDoubles = Array(repeating: 2.5, count: 3)
2   // anotherThreeDoubles is of type [Double], and equals [2.5,
    2.5, 2.5]
3
4   var sixDoubles = threeDoubles + anotherThreeDoubles
5   // sixDoubles is inferred as [Double], and equals [0.0, 0.0,
    0.0, 2.5, 2.5, 2.5]
```

Using The Array Literal To Create An Array:

Swift permits one to initialize an array by using the array literal, the array literal is the shortest form for one to write one or even more values of an array collection. The array literal consists of a collection of values. The values have been split using commas and enclosed with square brackets as shown below:

[value 1 , value 2 , value 3]

This example will create an array to store the values:

```
1   var shoppingList: [String] = ["Eggs", "Milk"]
2   // shoppingList has been initialized with two initial items
```

In the above example, we have declared a variable called shoppingList to be an array of string values. Since this array contains values which have been detailed to be of string type, it can only contain string values. In this case, we have the array initialized with two string values.

You should note that the "shoppingList" array has been created using the *var* keyword instead of the constant keyword *let* because additional items will be added to the array. In this example, we say the array literal has two String values. This resembles the "shoppingList variable declaration", and that is the reason why it is possible to assign the array literal as a means to make the array hold two initial values. As you can now see, with the "Swift's inference type "you should not worry so much with describing the array if you would like to initialize it using the array literal which contains the values similar type. The "shoppingList" list initialization could, therefore, be written in a short form as:

```swift
var shoppingList = ["Eggs", "Milk"]
```

Since we have all the values existing in the array literal of the same kind, Swift can refer to that [String] as the correct type for one apply for the "shoppingList" variable.

Access And Modify An Array:

Arrays in Swift are accessed and modified with the help of properties and methods. Or you can still use the subscript syntax. If you want to know how many items the array holds, the read only count is an important way to know:

```swift
print("The shopping list contains \(shoppingList.count) items.")
// Prints "The shopping list contains 2 items."
```

The Boolean isEmpty property allows one to perform a check to determine if the count property is equal to 0.

```swift
if shoppingList.isEmpty {
    print("The shopping list is empty.")
} else {
    print("The shopping list is not empty.")
}
// Prints "The shopping list is not empty."
```

You can add or create a new item at the end of the array by just calling the arrays append (_:) method:

```
1   shoppingList.append("Flour")
2   // shoppingList now contains 3 items, and someone is making pancakes
```

Then again, you can append an array to one of the most compatible items using the addition assignment symbol (+=):

```
1   shoppingList += ["Baking Powder"]
2   // shoppingList now contains 4 items
3   shoppingList += ["Chocolate Spread", "Cheese", "Butter"]
4   // shoppingList now contains 7 items
```

We extract a value from an array with the help of the subscript syntax, what we do is specify the index of the value which we want to extract inside the square brackets.

```
1   var firstItem = shoppingList[0]
2   // firstItem is equal to "Eggs"
```

Please note that in any array, the first item begins with the index 0 and not 1. Swift arrays are zero-indexed.

Again, the subscript construct allows you to modify the value of a specific index.

```
1   shoppingList[0] = "Six eggs"
2   // the first item in the list is now equal to "Six eggs" rather than "Eggs"
```

Whenever you choose to apply the subscript construct, the index which you will as??? has to be valid. For instance, if you decide to write shoppingList [shoppingList.count] = "Salt", it will result in a "runtime error".

You can further try to take advantage of the subscript syntax which will help you change the values immediately. The subscript syntax does not care whether the replacement set of values contains diverse length compared to the one being replaced. In the example below, we replace the "Chocolate Spread", "Cheese", and "Butter" with "Bananas" and "Apples".

```
1  shoppingList[4...6] = ["Bananas", "Apples"]
2  // shoppingList now contains 6 items
```

If your goal is to successfully insert an item into the array at a precise index, use the insert (_:at:) method:

```
1  shoppingList.insert("Maple Syrup", at: 0)
2  // shoppingList now contains 7 items
3  // "Maple Syrup" is now the first item in the list
```

The above call to the method insert will insert a new item having the value "Maple Syrup" at the start of the shopping list, shown by the 0 index.

Alternatively, you can do away with an item from the array using the method remove (at:). This method will do away with an item at a given index and still return it back.

```
1    let mapleSyrup = shoppingList.remove(at: 0)
2    // the item that was at index 0 has just been removed
3    // shoppingList now contains 6 items, and no Maple Syrup
4    // the mapleSyrup constant is now equal to the removed "Maple
       Syrup" string
```

Note:

If you attempt to change a value whose index does not fall inside the array's existing limits, you will activate a runtime error. You should first confirm whether an index is correct before you can proceed to compare the array's property *count*. The highest and correct index is the -1. This is because of the previous reason we mentioned array indexing. It starts from zero, but when the count is 0, it means we have no correct indexes.

If we have some gaps in the array, they get closed down when the item is removed. This means the value at the index 0 will be equal to "Six eggs".

The method removeLast () should allow you to eliminate the last item instead of the remove (at:) to avoid the chances of querying the array's count property.

```
1    let apples = shoppingList.removeLast()
2    // the last item in the array has just been removed
3    // shoppingList now contains 5 items, and no apples
4    // the apples constant is now equal to the removed "Apples"
       string
```

Iterate Over An Array:

The for-in loop is important when you want to iterate over a whole set of values using the for-in loop:

```
1    for item in shoppingList {
2            print(item)
3    }
4    // Six eggs
5    // Milk
6    // Flour
7    // Baking Powder
8    // Bananas
```

If you want the whole integer index for every item together with its value, you make use of the enumerated () method which will iterate the array. Every object array and the enumerated () method will create a tuple. The integers begin at zero and move up one for every item. If you opt to enumerate an entire array, the integer will match the item indices. However, you can choose to reduce the tuple and translate it into temporary constants as well as variables in the process of iteration.

```
1    for item in shoppingList {
2            print(item)
3    }
4    // Six eggs
5    // Milk
6    // Flour
7    // Baking Powder
8    // Bananas
```

Sets:

When we started to look at this Chapter, we discussed something about the set. If you can remember well, we said that it can store a collection of similar items without the presence of an organization. If order is not a big deal, then a set is one of the best to use. Sometimes, you can choose to use a set if the type of order for the items is not very important.

Hash Values - Set Types:

Set types should have the ability to be "hashable" so that it can allow items storage. The set type needs to offer a way for one to compute the hash value for itself. A hash value simply refers to that value which remains the same no matter the objects. This could be if c==d, then c.hashValue == d. hashValue.

In Swift, String, Bool and Double are some of the set types which are "hashable by default". The enumeration case values with no related values are hashable by default.

Another important point to remember is that we can convert the custom types to be dictionary types by aligning the custom types to the Swift protocols. The types which align to the hashable protocol need to have a gettable int feature referred to as hashValue. The value which is returned by the type's hashValue is not needed to be similar across many different implementations of the same program.

Since the Hashable property is Equitable, the types which conform to it should have the equals operator (==) implementation. The Equitable property requires the conforming nature of == to take the equivalence relation. This means, the implementation of the == has to fulfill the conditions below for all the values of the a, b and c.

- a==a
- a==b
- a==b && b == c meaning a == c

The Set Type Syntax:

Swift set type has the following construct "Set<Element>", in this situation Element is the type which the set allows to store. Unlike arrays, the sets will not permit an equivalent shorthand.

17

Creating And Initializing Empty Set

The syntax below will help you if you want to create and initialize empty set:

```
1    var letters = Set<Character>()
2    print("letters is of type Set<Character> with \(letters.count)
         items.")
3    // Prints "letters is of type Set<Character> with 0 items."
```

Meanwhile, let's assume that the context contains information. Then, it becomes easy to create an empty with the empty array literal.

```
1    letters.insert("a")
2    // letters now contains 1 value of type Character
3    letters = []
4    // letters is now an empty set, but is still of type
         Set<Character>
```

Creating A Set Using Array Literal:

It is possible to initialize a set by the help of an array literal. This is in fact one of the easiest ways to adopt if you want to quickly write more than one value from the set collection. You can look at the example below which creates a set favoriteGenres:

```
1    var favoriteGenres: Set<String> = ["Rock", "Classical", "Hip
         hop"]
2    // favoriteGenres has been initialized with three initial items
```

In this example, the favoriteGenres variable shall be declared as the "set of String Values". This is written as Set<String>. It is written this way because the set has a specific value type of String. It can only store String values. In this illustration, the "favoriteGenres se???? has been

18

initialized with the three String values which have been written inside the array literal.

Again, note that the "favoriteGenres" set has been declared as a variable but not a constant. The reason is the items are removed and added.

Chapter 3

Control Statements And Decisions In Loops

When we have a code implemented line after line, we call that sequential flow. With the sequential interruption, the code can be interrupted in several ways:

- You can use the flow controls. This refers to the code structures which will interfere with the general flow of the code. The term flow control describes the conditional statements and other different types of loops. Often, they divert the flow by making the app jump out of the current function. This forces the next line of code to perform a given action rather than the line of code located in the source file.

- By use of closures and functions. This refers to the part of the code which is executed as a response to specific conditions. Some of these conditions can include events or even certain references inside code which trigger asynchronous or synchronous processes. This will also interfere with the net-line structure to begin the procedure of responding to the event.

All the above concepts have different types of implementation based on the language used. This chapter will discuss some of the basic control statements in Swift to give you a head start.

Loops:

Every programming language has at least loops. Therefore, if Swift is not the first language you are learning, perhaps you have encountered loops at one point or the other while learning another computer programming language. Similar to other languages, Swift supports loops. However, you will see some slight difference when using loops in Swift. This is unique because it is not found in other languages.

We have two types of loops:

- The for loop which consists of a counter
- The while loop which depends on a specific condition

Again, we have another type of loop called polling loop. You may have used this one at one point in your life. The function of the poll loop is to confirm whether a certain action such as the button of the user's communication link is active or down. To implement a polling loop in Swift, the While loop helps you achieve that operation. However, kindly note that polling loops aren't that cheap. If you would like to monitor their conditions, they must be related to computer' resources.

The For Loop In Swift:

For loops exist in nearly every programming language. It forms the core of programming languages. One reason for this is that the for loop command will allow you to implement certain parts of your code in a repeated manner depending on control.

In Swift, we have two types of for loops:

- The for-in loops
- The for-condition-increment

We shall look at the above types of for loop in the next sections.

Don't think the above for loops are new. No! In fact, they existed since the start of computer languages. However, you will realize that the for-in type of loop is mostly associated with the object-oriented programming. Still, if this is not your first time learning programming, for-in loops should not be new to you. We shall learn more about the for-in loops compared to other loops because they aren't that common. In addition, Swift developers find themselves using it regularly compared to other loops.

We Start With The For-In Loops:

Even though they might appear new, they aren't. The for-in loops are not new to Swift programming. They are applied in many other object oriented languages such as C++. They are important when you want to work with a collection of objects. Instead of objects indexed in arrays.

Array objects tend to have a definite sequence. In other words, we can't have array elements holding the same index. If choose to create a for loop which will process every array element, then you should take advantage of the for loop. It is one of the best approaches to follow.

However, it happens sometimes when you have a collection of items that the objects aren't indexed and in no particular order. We can look at it like the objects or elements are in a random order. In this kind of situation, the objects are said to belong to a specific collection. Furthermore, the objects get identified individually using different methods rather than the index. There are also certain situations where the individual objects aren't identified because of how difficult it is.

Flicking through an array in a random order is very annoying, but in big situations, the order of presentation is not necessary. Your goal is to handle every appointment, every friend or bank account. As long as you are going to access every element and remove none, you are good to go.

The idea behind the syntax of for-in loop depends on two protocols:

- Generator
- Sequence

The Generator has a next function which is the main core. Now, anyone who has a class or creates a class which contains the sequence protocol will have the ability to access the next function which can now be adopted by the iterator. Regardless of the way the next function shall be ordered, it is upon the decision of the class or structure. This means it could either be random or ordered. Looking from a higher level of Swift perspective, the next is not defined. In real life, next is associated with contexts such as "next candidate in line", "next session" and so forth. When writing your Swift code, it is encouraged to imagine that we have no pre-arranged order unless you are sure that we have one.

The basic syntax to use for-in loops:

```
for <item> in <collection> {
   <statements>
}
```

You should not misinterpret the italicized terms as part of them, they are just basic descriptions which point to missing syntax elements. They consist of:

- <item> This one will point to a specific object in the collection. It holds a different element for every loop evaluation.

- <collection> This can contain any class or structure which assumes the nature of the sequence protocol. Don't even care to search it in the Swift documentation.

- <statements> These point to the code statements in Swift.

The steps below create a code which you can test with for-in type of loop:

1. Create a collection which belongs to the for-in loop. You can do that by declaring statements such as:

```
var elements = [1, 3, 5, 17, -1]
```

In the above example, our declared collection is a variable. However, it could be of any other type, not necessarily a variable.

2. Now, create the for-in loop. Look at this example:

```
for myElement in elements {
   // do something with myElement
}
```

You remember that this is a loop declaration. No need to have a different declaration for the myElement. If you do so, you shall have declared a separate variable. This loop will then work on the collection you had referenced in the first step. In this case, the myElement will contain every value of the loop. So, you can still use it inside the loop. The following are some of the for-in loops variations:

- To carry out a trial on a given item. Usually, you do a test on an item but you can also make use of it as an operation. There are times when you can carry out both. For instance, when the code below is placed inside the loop, it determines if the value of the iterated element can be a negative number. It will print out that particular value:

```
if myElement < 0 {
   println ( " \(myElement.description) is a negative
      number")
}
```

- Breaking out from a loop. Let's say that you are scanning a collection by looking for the lowest or even highest numeric value, you'll need to search all the values in the collection. This means that this kind of variation won't be of much help. Meanwhile, if you want to determine a specific value or even a value which will satisfy a given condition, this is the best to use. When carrying out this search, you'll want to stop once you find what you have been looking for. To end the loop from that point, you need to add the break statement. This statement will exit you from the loop and continue execution on the next line. Here is an example:

```
if myElement < 0 {
  println ( " \(myElement.description) is a negative
    number")
  break;
}
```

- **Finding Every Item In Each Iteration:** As you might remember, the item in every for-in loop has the element from the collection. This element can be a value, as it has been indicated in the code below, but still, it can be an object. In the example of an ordered collection, like an array, you might want to know the index of an element number. Since this kind of information does not belong to the for-in loop, you will have to calculate it. To carry out the calculation, you will have to create a counter. This counter will build a special value for every element inside the loop. Here are the steps to follow if you want to create one:

1. Declare counter variable outside the loop. Ensure that the variable is declared using var, but not with let. You can do it this way: *var index = 2*

2. While within the loop, perform a counter increment: index ++

Now, here is how the body of your loop will be:

```
var index = 0
if myElement < 0 {
  println ( " \(myElement.description) at \(index) is
    a negative number")
}
index++
```

- **Ignore the item:** In some cases, you don't really need to modify the item returned from every iteration. In the above case, you can choose to replace it with an underscore character as shown below:

For _in elements {

But, just in case you would like to reference the item later, you should apply the technique described previously.

- **Dictionary iteration:**

It is possible to do a dictionary iteration the same way you can iterate any other collection. The only variation happens when the item located in the syntax is a tuple consisting of a key and value for the dictionary element. Here is how a for-in loop for a dictionary will appear:

```
for (myKey, myValue) in myDictionary {
    //do something with myKey and myValue
}
```

Here is a code which uses the for-in loop to control a collection of items:

```
// Playground - noun: a place where people can play
var elements = [1, 3, 5, 17, -1]
var index = 0;
for myElement in elements {
    // do something with myElement
    if myElement < 0 {
        println ( " \(myElement.description) at \(index.description) is a negative number")
    }
    index++
}
```

Now, Let's Turn Our Attention To The For-Condition-Increment Loops

As you know the for-condition–increment is the basis of for statements if you have learned another different programming language. When it comes to Swift for-condition loops, there is no difference. It is more or less the same as other languages with only one distinction. You don't have to place the loop control in the parentheses. You can have it, but it is not supposed to be. The general construct for the for-condition–increment is:

```
for <initialization>; <condition>; <increment>{
   <statements>
}

for <initialization>; <condition>; <increment>{
   <statements>
}
```

Similar to the for-in loop, we have some components which should not be confused with the syntax of the for-condition. For instance, the < and > aren't part of the syntax. Others include:

- <Initialization>: This simply initializes the counter. You should declare the index counter before you use it.

- <condition>: It will specify the condition based on the way the counter continues to increment. This type of condition is evaluated for each cycle in the loop, then the counter is incremented until the point when the condition fails.

- <increment>: This describes the expression one should use to increase the counter. The most common increment is the myCounter ++, which will increase the counter by 1, still, you can choose any type of increment you want.

- <statements>: These often point to the Swift code statements.

An example of how the for-condition loop is applied in code is shown below:

```
for (myElementCounter=0; myElementCounter <5;
    myElementCounter ++) {
```

You can choose to include the parenthesis but you don't have to. A more practical example is shown below:

```
// Playground - noun: a place where people can play
var elements = [1, 3, 5, 17, -1]
var myElementCounter = 0;
for myElementCounter =0; myElementCounter <5;
  myElementCounter ++ {
    // do something with myElement
    if elements[myElementCounter] > 15 {
        println (  " \(elements[myElementCounter].description)
          at \( myElementCounter.description) is greater than
          15")
    }
}
```

Swift While Loops:

Similar to other languages, Swift has While loops. The basic syntax for the Swift while loops only needs a condition. Here is how it looks:

```
while myValue < 10 {
    // do something
}
```

If we review the above loop, myValue becomes the condition. Don't forget that you need to alter the value of myValue. If it does not change and the loop continues to run, the loop may be infinite. You should also underline that the condition in a while loop can at times be an expression. This means that a while loop can resemble the for-conditioning-increment loop in certain cases.

```
var myValue = 5
while myValue++ < 10 {
    // do something
}
```

Here, you should notice that there are three components of the for-condition-increment. It is the declaration of the myValue as well as the initial value. In Swift, it should have the initialization, condition and increment. The while loops exist in two forms:

- Do while loop. You must have come across this while learning another programming language. With the following form, often the action gets executed at least once before the condition. It takes the form of a do < action > while <condition>

- While<condition> do < action>. In this type of while loop, we have our condition evaluated first. Now, when the condition is found to be true, the action will be performed.

All the above types of while conditions are the same in the way they are applied in other languages. The only exception could be that the condition defined in other languages has to within the parentheses.

Conditions In Swift

In the Swift language, the if statements are used and applied in a similar fashion as other languages but there are some changes when it comes to the switch statements.

The If Statements

Sometimes, you should realize that it is easy to talk about if statements because how they are used in other languages is the same in Swift. The syntax includes:

```
if <condition> {
   <statements>
}
```

In the same fashion, an if –else statement will have two branches:

```
if <condition> {
   <statements for true>
} else {
   <statements for false>
}
```

The greatest distinction is in the way the Swift language applies the if statement. You don't need to place the condition within the parentheses.

Still, you can have it, but no need to place it. One other difference is that the condition in swift can assume a Boolean expression or variable of any kind which takes the BooleanType convention. It is not easy to identify the above differences by just looking at the syntax examples.

Switch Statements:

The basic syntax of the switch statement includes:

```
switch <control expression> {
   case <pattern 1>:
      <statements>
   case <pattern 2> where <condition>:
      <statements>
   case <pattern 3> where <condition,
         <pattern 4> where condition>:
      <statements>
   default:
      <statements>
}
```

As I said before, Switch statements in Swift tend to have certain variations from Switch statements in other computer programming languages. The list of differences highlights some of the issues developers have experienced over the years while working with the C-type switch statements. These issues are solved with the help of the features in Swift:

- Falling through: Every developer has encountered this situation. In most languages, you must include the break statement, not unless control jumps to the following case statement. However, the Swift switch statement solves this by passing the control to the first statement that comes after the switch statement.

- Exhaustiveness: In the Swift switch statement, the statement has to go round all potential value for the control expression. But still, you can achieve this goal by using a default case.
- Guard clause: Swift allows you to have a guard statement which starts with the where. What this means is that you can have more than one case statement which matches a single control expression value. The guard clause resembles the AND statement. It enhances the basic case statement using extra aspects.

Transferring Control:

Swift still has some transfer statements. The continue and break statement are not different from the other languages such as PHP, C, and Java.

- Continue: You are free to apply the continue statement in whichever type of loop statements described in this Chapter. It puts an end to a specific iteration and moves to the next.
- Break: It will end a loop iteration. Control switches back to the initial statement after the switch statement.
- Fallthrough: With this statement, it emulates the property of the case statements within the switch statement. If it has been located within a switch statement, then control is passed to next case.

Chapter 4

Swift Functions

Before we can begin to look at Functions in Swift, I want you to remember those days you were a high school kid. But this time, I want you to try and recall the topic of algebra. I believe you weren't sleeping during that lesson, but paying attention. Well, if you can recall well, your mathematics teacher introduced and explained the topic of function. In mathematics, you came to learn that a function is a mathematical formula which accepts some inputs, performs certain operations and produces a given output.

The most important components of a function include:

- The name
- The input
- The expression
- The result

Most functions are written in the mathematical form. However, they can still be described in the human natural language.

Writing Functions in Swift Language:

Swift's syntax for functions is a bit different from the mathematical functions. The overall syntax includes:

```
func funcName(paramName : type, ...) -> returnType
```

You should look at the example below to help you understand the syntax of functions in Swift:

```
// Playground - noun: a place where people can play

import Cocoa

var str = "Chapter 4 Playground"

func fahrenheitToCelsius(fahrenheitValue : Double) -> Double {
    var result : Double
    
    result = (((fahrenheitValue - 32) * 5) / 9)
    
    return result
}
```

From the above example, there is something new which you need to learn on line 7. The "func" keyword helps Swift developers to declare a swift function. The declaration takes the name of the function, independent name of the variable or a parameter name surrounded by parentheses.

After the parameter, we have two characters which imply that this specific type of function should return a value of Double type. Next, there is the opening curly brace which identifies the start of a function. On line 8, we have declared a Double type of variable called result. This will store the value which will??? the result of the function. You should realize that it is similar to the function's return type previously declared on line 7.

We have the initial mathematical function written on line 10 together with the *result* of the expression. On line 12, we have the result taken back to the caller with the return keyword. Any moment you would want to exit a function and go back to the return calling party, the keyword *return* becomes useful.

Now, we want to call the function we have created. In your text editor, type the below lines of code and watch out the results in the Results sidebar:

```
var outdoorTemperatureInFahrenheit = 88.2
var outdoorTemperatureInCelsius = fahrenheitToCelsius(outdoorTemperature
→ InFahrenheit)
```

From the above screenshot, we have declared a new variable called *outdoorTemperatureInFahrenheit* and assigned it a value. Remember that Swift refers the type in the above example to be of Double. The value is later transferred to line 16 where there is a function. Here, a new variable called *outdoorTemperatureInCelsius* is then declared. On the output sidebar, we see a value with repeating decimal to be the result of the function. If you review the result, you will notice that 32.2222 degrees Celsius is equal to the 88.2 degrees Fahrenheit. Now, you can sit back and relax as you enjoy using your temperature conversion tool.

Well, if you have followed closely what we have done on this particular example. You should give yourself a trial by writing the inverse of the method with the help of this formula.

$$f(x) = \frac{x \cdot 9}{5} + 32$$

Move on and try to code it up by yourself. Once you have finished coding up, you should compare it with the code below:

```
func celsiusToFahrenheit(celsiusValue : Double) -> Double {
    var result : Double

    result = (((celsiusValue * 9) / 5) + 32)

    return result
}

outdoorTemperatureInFahrenheit = celsiusToFahrenheit(outdoorTemperature
-> InCelsius)
```

The method on line 18-24 converts the Celsius to Fahrenheit and returns a value. You can see that if we pass the previous Celsius value we get the Fahrenheit value.

Here, you have successfully built two Swift functions which perform something important. You should try and play around with other values.

Not Just Numbers Alone:

Swift function goes beyond the mathematical concept we have seen above. In a wider perspective, the functions are flexible and strong enough to accommodate more than one parameter. In addition, it can accept types rather than numeric types.

Let's consider writing a Swift function which will accept more than one parameter and return a value rather than a double.

```
func buildASentence(subject : String, verb : String, noun : String) -> String
    return subject + " " + verb + " " + noun + "!"
}

buildASentence("Swift", "is", "cool")
buildASentence("I", "love", "languages")
```

Once you are through with typing, you need to review your work. You should notice that we have declared a new function buildASentence, which holds three parameters. All the parameters belong to the string types. The function will also return a String type too. Line 29 holds the line which returns the result.

To be clear, we have the function called both on line 32 and 33. This outputs the results in the output sidebar. You should be free to use your own values for the parameters.

36

Paremeters AD NAUSEAM

Can you visualize creating a life changing banking application for the Apple, and you would want to develop a means to add some random number of certain account balances. You just want to create a Swift function which will perform the addition. The challenge you are facing is that you aren't sure the number of accounts which you want to be added up at a specific time. The trick to use is the Swift's variable parameter passing syntax.

```
// Parameters Ad Nauseam
func addMyAccountBalances(balances : Double...) -> Double {
    var result : Double = 0

    for balance in balances {
        result += balance
    }
```

```
        return result
}

addMyAccountBalances(77.87)
addMyAccountBalances(10.52, 11.30, 100.60)
addMyAccountBalances(345.12, 1000.80, 233.10, 104.80, 99.90)
```

The function's Parameter is better called variadic parameter because it has the ability to represent an unknown number of parameters.

If you look at line 36, we have our balances parameter declared to be of type double. It is followed by (...) and a return of type double. The existence of the ellipsis makes Swift to know that there should be another parameter of type double when the function gets called. The function call runs from line 4-48. For every call, the function had a different value.

First Class Functions:

This is one of the unique and outstanding things with Swift functions. They are simply first-class objects. Hope that looks interesting? First-class objects provide one with the capability to deal with a function just like any other ordinary value. The choice is yours, either opt to assign a function to a variable or even a constant to become a parameter to the next function. Let's use the illustration of what happens in a bank. We have cash withdrawal and cash deposit. Right?

Let's say that every Monday, you deposit a specific amount and then when the week nears to end you withdraw a different amount. The code below gives you the example of how this scenario is implemented:

```swift
var account1 = ( "State Bank Personal", 1011.10 )
var account2 = ( "State Bank Business", 24309.63 )

func deposit(amount : Double, account : (name : String, balance : Double)) ->
    (String, Double) {
    var newBalance : Double = account.balance + amount
    return (account.name, newBalance)
}
```

```
func withdraw(amount : Double, account : (name : String, balance : Double)) ->
  (String, Double) {
    var newBalance : Double = account.balance - amount
    return (account.name, newBalance)
}

let mondayTransaction = deposit
let fridayTransaction = withdraw

let mondayBalance = mondayTransaction(300.0, account1)
let fridayBalance = fridayTransaction(1200, account2)
```

In this example, we have created two accounts both on line 77 and 88. Every account is a tuple comprising of an account balance and account name. Line 80 we declare a function called deposit which takes two types of parameters:

- The tuple called account
- The amount called Double

40

The tuple consists of two members:

- Name-type string

- Balance –type double-shows the funds in the account

The tuple type has still been declared as the return type.

We go to line "81", we have declared a variable to show new balance. The variable holds the total of the account tuple plus the amount passed by the variable. The result of the tuple is created on line 82 and then returned.

When you turn to line 90 and 91, there are two new constants declared and allocated to functions respectively by name: withdraw and deposit. Given that we deposit the money on Monday, this transaction is passed to the deposit function. The same happens for the withdrawals, we make withdrawals on Friday, therefore, the Friday transaction is passed the Withdraw function.

The lines "93 and 94" will output the results of both transactions. The results sidebar has the results.

"Throw me a function"

The same way we have a function which can return String, int or Double. "A function can also return another function". You can check the lines of code below:

```
func chooseTransaction(transaction: String) -> (Double, (String, Double)) ->
    (String, Double) {
    if transaction == "Deposit" {
        return deposit
    }

    return withdraw
}
```

The function chooseTransaction accepts a String as the parameter, which it then applies it to determine the banking transaction type. The same function will return a function, the function accepts a tuple of String, Double, and String. Now, let's examine this code in close proximity. First, the line opens with the function definition and one single parameter. Next, we have characters which have to hold the return type value.

Then, the return type which is, in reality, has two: the tuple of Double, double and String together with the return function of the characters.

Finally, we have the "return type", which consist of a tuple of String and Double.

In the figure above, we have two functions on line 80 and 85. The two functions are bank transactions which we saw previously. They contain the function definition which takes two parameters and later has a return tuple which is comprised of the double and string.

On line 97, we have a comparison taking place of the transaction parameter string against "Deposit" string and in case we have a match found, the deposit function is given back on line 98. Now, we have two functions which have the ability to output two functions. How do you apply it"? You could be asking yourself that question or perhaps you are wondering whether you apply the function in another variable then call it? Well, here is the solution:

```
// option 1: capture the function in a constant and call it
let myTransaction = chooseTransaction("Deposit")
myTransaction(225.33, account2)

// option 2: call the function result directly
chooseTransaction("Withdraw")(63.17, account1)
```

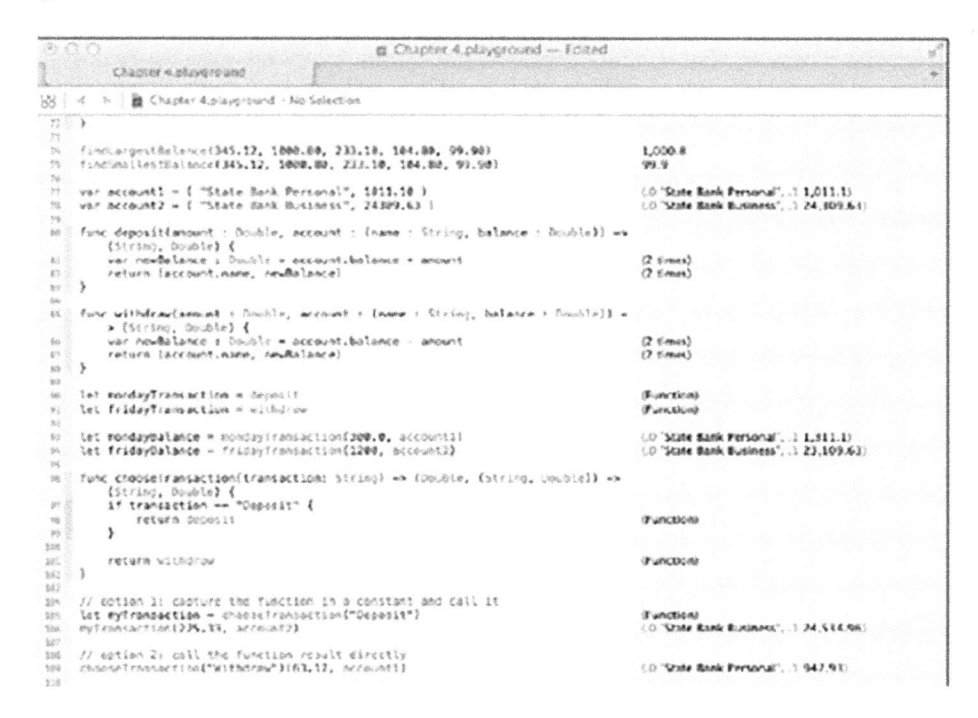

Get time and review the screenshot above especially on line 105. You should manage to identify the returned function. The function has later been called at line 106.

43

There is an alternate style on line 109. Here, we have the "chooseTransaction function" called to accept access to the withdraw function. Rather than letting a constant hold the result, the returned function gets instantly pressed into a service using parameters.

Function In A Function:

So far, you understand the concept of "functions returned by functions" which is later given to constants. Now, let's look at declaring a function within another function. This is known as nested functions. If you have heard of nested loops, then the same concept will apply with some little variations.

First, why are nested functions important? Good question. Whenever you would like to hide, isolate a particular functionality which does not require to get exposed to the outer layers. You can look at the screenshot below:

```
// nested function example
func bankVault(passcode : String) -> String {
    func openBankVault(Void) -> String {
        return "Vault opened"
    }
```

```
func closeBankVault(Void) -> String {
    return "Vault closed"
}
    if passcode == "secret" {
        return openBankVault()
    }
    else {
        return closeBankVault()
    }
}

println(bankVault("wrongsecret"))
println(bankVault("secret"))
```

When you review line 112, we have a new function, bankVault defined. It takes a single parameter of String type and later return a String.

On line 113 and 116, there are two types of function:

- OpenBankVault

- CloseBankVault

The above two functions don't take a parameter or return a String.

When we go to line 119, we have the "passcode parameter" compared with the string "secret". Suppose a match is found, bank vault gets opened by the call of the OpenBankVault function. If not, the bank vault will remain closed.

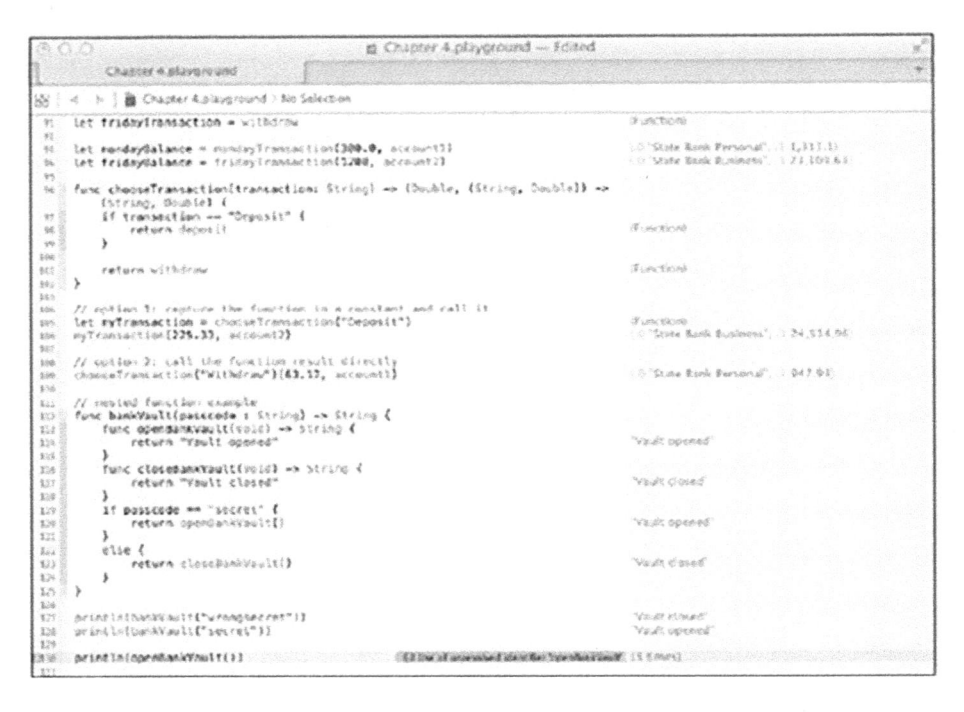

If look at line 113 and 116, we have a new Swift keyword: Void. This is the same in other languages. It generally means "emptiness". We use the Void keyword as a placeholder when we declare empty parameter lists.

Between the lines 127 and 128, the code will output the results of the method both the correct and incorrect passcode. You should just pay attention that "OpenBankVault and CloseBankVault function" are encircled by a function, and they remain unknown when we jump outside the function.

In general, the greatest advantage with nesting functions is the protection of functions. You should always apply nested functions anytime you want to have functions which work together. You can look at the picture below to develop a much better understanding of the concepts.

Default Parameters:

So far you have learned a ton of important topics about Swift functions. You have seen how to apply it in the code. As you may have discovered, Swift functions give you a great ability to develop real-world solutions to daily problems. Still, we have another intriguing feature which Swift functions provide us with. This is called the default parameter values. It will give you the freedom to create functions which hold a parameter that has a "prefilled" value.

Take, for example, a developer who would want to build a function which can create checks. This function will have two parameters: the amount and the person to whom the check has to reach. Obviously, in a real-world scenario, these are the crucial aspects of the information which you would want to know. However, in the meantime, you should imagine a function which can take the default payee and later the amount just in case there is not information relayed. Below you will see an example of the above description:

```
func writeCheck(payee : String = "Unknown", amount : String = "10.00") ->
-> String {
    return "Check payable to " + payee + " for $" + amount
}

writeCheck()
writeCheck(payee : "Donna Soileau")
writeCheck(payee : "John Miller", amount : "45.00")
```

You notice the way we have defined the function:

```
func writeCheck(payee : String = "Unknown", amount : String = "10.00") ->
-> String
```

Now, only one thing remains and that is the passing of the parameters actual values. In the above example, we are assigning the payee with "Unknown" as the default while amount has been set to "10.00". This is the approach to use in Swift programming when you want to have a function assume the default parameters. Simply assign the parameter with the value name.

Well, how does one call such a function? There are basically three ways of doing it as shown in the same code:

- You pass no parameters when you call the function
- You pass a single parameter
- You pass both parameters

So, in the first scenario where we don't have any parameters passed, we use the default values defined to show the returned string. In the cases which have remained, we have the values which have been passed applied in the default values.

Don't forget that whenever you want to call a function declared to accept the default parameters, it is vital to pass both the name of the parameter and colon. With default parameters, you experience the flexibility of making use of a known value rather than passing it explicitly. But, they aren't applicable for every function.

What is contained in the name?

You know how easy it is to declare functions in Swift language? But, how about if I told you that parameters in Swift language can accept not only a text once defined by the func keyword? This is to mean that for every Swift parameter, there is an optional "external parameter" which occurs before the name of the parameter. The external names simply improve the clarity and function description.

```
func writeCheck(payer : String, payee : String, amount : Double) -> String {
    return "Check payable from \(payer) to \(payee) for $\(amount)"
}

writeCheck("Dave Johnson", "Coz Fontenot", 1000.0)
```

[screenshot of Chapter 4.playground code in Xcode]

The above function is not similar to the previous functions between lines 130 -132. Here are the differences:

- We have an extra parameter called payer to determine the source of the check

- There are no default parameters

If you review line 142, you will discover that the function "writeCheck" has three parameters. Just by looking at the name of the function, you can easily predict the function. If you are going to do a guess, a correct guess is that the parameter double is the amount. However, if you don't take time to look or familiarize yourself with the function declaration, you will not realize what the two parameter Strings are?

Using an external parameter, it will help offer a solution to this problem by providing an extra name to every parameter which needs to be passed whenever the function is called. This will make it appear clear to everyone who will read the code.

```
func writeBetterCheck(from payer : String, to payee : String, total amount :
 Double) -> String {
    return "Check payable from \(payer) to \(payee) for $\(amount)"
}

writeBetterCheck(from : "Fred Charlie", to: "Ryan Hanks", total : 1350.0)
```

Chapter 5

Structures and Classes in Swift

Classes in Swift resemble classes in other languages. But, one exception with classes in Swift is that they aren't the only ones which can produce the behaviors of classes. And this is the unique difference between Swift and many other languages.

Both the structure and enumeration of the Swift can have several methods the same way classes are. What this now implies is that whenever you want to perform a restructuring of your Swift app, you will require to re-evaluate some of your earlier decisions concerning what really makes up for class objects. There are situations when the structure and enumeration are needed.

We shall guide you on the basics of working with structures, classes, and enumerations in the Swift language. Since they are closely similar in Swift, we shall look at them as one.

Classes, Structures, and Enumerations:

Having classes, enumerations and structures in Swift together show the similarities which they share. However, there is one specific difference which you need to pay attention to:

- Structures and enumeration are types of values.

This means that an instance of enumerations and structures are emulated whenever they are passed into a given function or allocated to a constant. As a result, there is a possibility of having many copies of the structure and enumeration, and for each copy, it contains its own unique values.

Meanwhile, classes are "reference types". So, when a class is allocated to a variable, we have a reference to the instance transferred. Since we have one instance which has been transferred to the variables, a modification of the values of the respectful instance takes place across all the specified copies.

You can look at the table below which has some of the features present in enumerations, classes and structures.

Features in Classes, Structures, and Enumerations			
Feature	*Classes*	*Structures*	*Enumerations*
Instances	X	X	X
Properties	X	X	computed properties only
Methods	X	X	X
Subscripts	X	X	X
Initializers	X	X	X
Extensions	X	X	X
Protocols	X	X	X
Inheritance	X		
Type casting	X		
Deinitializers	X		
ARC	X		

- Instances-An instance refers to an object which is the real representation of the class. There are specific object oriented languages where the class can still act as the instance.

- Properties-It upon your choice to either create properties which can be computed or stored when they are needed.

- Subscripts- It is possible to create subscripts which will allow you to gain access to specific features of an instance type depending on the subscript logic. Some of the examples consist of the multiple indexing types which belong to the multi-dimensional object. In some cases, they are retrieved just like they are a one-dimensional array. You can also use many dimensions.

- Initializers-This will help one prepare properties for a new instance.

- Protocols-it is possible to create methods inside a protocol which should be implemented using an object which mirrors the protocol.

- Extensions-The extensions will give you the ability to add properties and methods without the presence of the code which you want to add them.

- Inheritance-A class can inherit from another class with the help of a subclass. A class can contain any different amounts of subclasses.

- Deinitializers-This will help you to conduct a clean-up, especially of a class instance, want to be deallocated.

- The type Casting-It is possible to treat one class or sub class as a condition.

- ARC- This will permit one to have many instances of a class.

Class Declaration:

This section will review some of the inner tasks of the structures, enumeration and class in Swift. The picture below indicates that majority of the code in Swift exists in the master view controller. This is the view which allows one to start and delete events. The "master view controller" will exchange communication with the detail view controller in the right side.

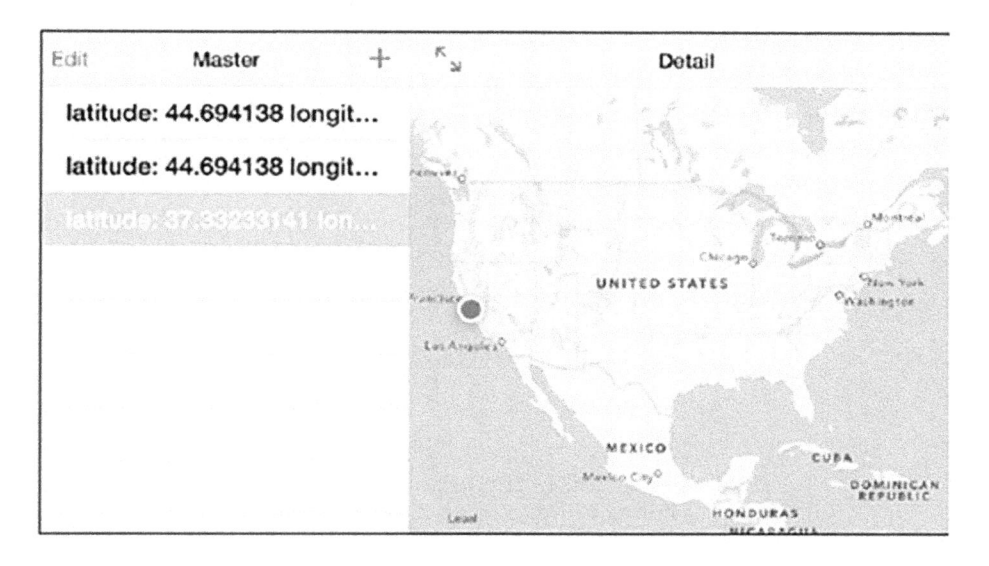

Detailed view controller often is executed using a simple class called DetailViewController. Because of the way this class is simple, we encourage you to take time and look at it so that you can develop the right notion of how classes operate.

In the figure below, we have the DetailViewController. From there, you should be able to realize that we have nothing complicated in the code, you should be fine with reading and understanding the whole class.

```swift
import UIKit
import MapKit

class DetailViewController: UIViewController {

    //@IBOutlet weak var detailDescriptionLabel: UILabel!
    @IBOutlet var mapView: MKMapView!


    var detailItem: AnyObject? {
        didSet {
            // Update the view.
            self.configureView()
        }
    }

    func configureView() {
        // Update the user interface for the detail item.
        /*if let detail: AnyObject = self.detailItem {
            if let label = self.detailDescriptionLabel {
                label.text =
             detail.valueForKey("timeStamp")!.description
            }
        }*/
    }

    override func viewDidLoad() {
        super.viewDidLoad()
```

Continuation:

```swift
        // Do any additional setup after loading
            the view, typically from a nib.
        self.configureView()
    }

    override func didReceiveMemoryWarning() {
        super.didReceiveMemoryWarning()
        // Dispose of any resources that can be
            recreated.
    }
}
```

The next section examines the code above in much detail so that you get familiar with the concept of Swift classes. What you need to realize is that many Swift classes go beyond what you have seen above, however, they all take this form.

A file of Swift will contain a class, an enumeration file, and a structure in any particular order.

Import Declarations:

In Swift class, we have the section for declaring imports, which will import frameworks. Any time you are going to build an XCode class file for the Swift, you will have to place the import declaration.

Let's say you are not working in Swift but Objective –C. You will insert this statement in your file.

```
#import <Foundation/Foundation.h>
```

You should be careful to realize that the Objective C is a bit different. In Swift, we have the import declaration while for the Objective C is simply a compiler directive. Again in Swift, you will perform the import by using its actual name. When you turn to the OS X, we do the import by using both the name and the interface file. In reality, you should not have any worries concerning the import because they are already set up for you. Even if you don't see it there, you already have a template which you can adopt.

Declaring A Class:

You have so far seen how we declare a class in Swift, it occupies a big space of the class declaration. You should be able to identify the first and last line of your class declaration. If you aren't sure, look at the example below:

```
class DetailViewController: UIViewController {
}
```

Subclass Declaration:

You have seen that when we want to declare a class we need to begin with the class keyword which is followed by the class name, a colon and superclass name. If we go back to the code above, we can identify DetailViewController as the name of the class. This is a subclass of the UIViewController. Don't forget that there can only exist one superclass unless there is none.

Base Class Declaration:

So far you have learned how to declare classes in swift, how to declare subclass and a superclass. But, what about the base class? Well, if you want to declare a base class. What you simply do is to remove the colon and the name of the superclass. Remember that a base class is a type of class without the superclass. Let's assume that DetailViewController was a base class, then, this is how we could have proceeded with the base class declaration:

```
class DetailViewController
```

Using A Protocol:

If you have a class which will use more than one protocol, then they should be outlined after the superclass if it is present. If not, it should simply follow the colon.

How To Declare A Subclass And Use A Protocol?

This is how it is done:

```
class DetailViewController: UIViewController, MyProtocol
```

Base Class And Protocol:

```
class DetailViewController: MyProtocol
```

As you can see, you require the colon if you have both the protocol and superclass. If you have a base class which does not have a protocol, it does not need a colon.

When you have finished with class declaration, you need to place the body of your class inside the brackets.

Declaration Of The Structure:

Where we have reached so far, declaring a structure is not a hard thing. They are just similar to the way we have done the classes. The only exception to pay attention to when declaring your structure is that they should not have a superclass. The only things which you need to describe are the protocols which are adopted by the structure.

Declaring enum:

The same with a class, an enumeration declaration must begin with the enum keyword. Then you should follow with the name of the enum, then put a colon and if you have protocols you should include them. As you can see, this takes a similar approach to the way we did for the classes. However, there is only one possible scenario for a superclass. This is because enum does not inherit from another one. Below you can see an example of an enum declaration:

Enum MyHouse {

Just like structures and classes, the enum should also begin with capital letter.

Now, let's look at the body of an enum. The enum body should comprise of cases which are separated by commas. Every case should have a unique name. It could also describe more about the type of values it holds.

```
enum MyAnimals {
    case dog, cat, horse, cow
}
```

Components and Subcomponents:

One of the popular applications of Swift enumeration involves the switch statement. Both of these two elements are very powerful in the Swift programming language, and they work in unison. You can take a look at a switch statement which makes use of enumeration:

```
enum MyAnimal {
    case dog, cat, horse, cow
}

var myPet = MyAnimal.cat

switch myPet {
case .cow:
   println ("moo")
case .cat :
   println ("meow")
case .dog:
   println ("woof")
case .horse:
   println ("neigh")
default:
   println ("silence")
}
```

You should play around with the above code to find out some of the results you get when you decide to alter the var statement. You will realize that we have a default statement since, with Swift, the switch statement is exhaustive. As an experiment, try to delete it and you will notice that you don't get any error because you have covered all possibilities.

You should attempt to add a donkey to become part of the cases. This will trigger an error message since the cases are not exhaustive. You should try to adddonkey or even a place a default case.

Again, you should try and add some raw integer values to the enumeration to make it appear more traditional. You can have a look at a different way to write the enumeration.

```
enum MyAnimal2:Int {
    case dog = 1, cat, horse = 3, cow
}
```

However, if you would like to declare an int type of enumeration, you need to try and access the raw values with the help of rawValue function using this form:

```
var myPet2 = MyAnimal2.cat.rawValue
```

The Body:

When we examine the structure, class or enumeration, you often see methods inside the body, other times it is the properties and in some cases the variables. Besides the properties, functions and instance variables, classes have both actions and outlets. In other words, they are properties associated to storyboard elements. The process of creating the relation to the storyboard elements is the point at which it links your code to the user interface objects.

The UI Actions And The Outlets For Classes Alone:

If they do exist, they carry this general construct:

```
@IBOutlet var mapView: MKMapView!
```

Chapter 6

Making Better Swift Apps

The Swift language was introduced in the September of 2014. Swift has language properties which improve the safety of the developer's code as well as make them code faster and in a manner which is reliable as compared to using the Objective-C. In this section, we share with you some tips on how to make better apps using the Swift language. These tips will help you build clean as well as help developers who are much conversant with the Objective-C to understand even the Swift language better. Here you will get tips for different levels, regardless of whether you are just starting out in the Swift language.

Tips:

Enhance The Readability Of The Constants:
One of the best ways you can make use of structs in the Swift language is to build a file which has all the constants. This is very important because the language will allow you to create nested structures such as:

```
import Foundation

struct Constants {
    struct FoursquareApi {
        static let BaseUrl = "https://api.foursquare.com/v2/"
    }
    struct TwitterApi {
        static let BaseUrl = "https://api.twitter.com/1.1/"
    }
    struct Configuration {
        static let UseWorkaround = true
    }
}
```

This type of nesting provides a namespace for the constants. For example, you can use the Constants FoursquareApi.BaseUrl to gain entry to the Foursquare's BaseUrl constant. This helps improve the readability and offers an extra layer to perform encapsulation.

Keep away from "NSObject and @objc" to enhance the performance

By providing support to the Objective-C runtime makes the method calls to use automatic dispatch rather than the static dispatch. The overall effect is that the methods which help the "Objective-C runtime" will develop a four times performance boost.

Make Use Of The Swizzling Method In Swift

This is a technique which replaces one method execution with another. Swift will enhance the code so that it can make a direct memory reference of searching up for the method location at the runtime as in the Objective-C. This means, Swizzling can't work in Swift classes, not unless:

- ExtendNSObject. You should not attempt this unless you are doing it for the swizzling method. It is very important to note that the swizzling method will operate on preexisting classes which contain the NSobject as part of their base class, however, we are much better using dynamic to select methods.

- Disable this optimization using the "dynamic keyword". This is the right choice and the option which is sensible especially when the codebase is fully in Swift.

- Make use of the @obj annotation on the swizzled method. This is right mostly when the method which you want to swizzle has been accessed by the objective-c.

Tips For New Beginners In Swift

You Should Make It A Practice To Clean Up Your Asynchronous Code:

Swift has one of the best syntaxes for one to write ending functions. Perhaps, if you have learned Objective-C, you will agree with me that we have completion blocks in the Objective –C. However, they were introduced later on, and their syntax was not really nice. As you can see below:

```
[self loginViaHttpWithRequest:request completionBlockWithSuccess:^(LoginOperation
    [self showMainScreen];
} failure:^(LoginOperation *operation, NSError *error) {
    [self showFailedLogin];
}];
```

Fortunately, Swift will make everything simple with the beautiful syntax.

```
loginViaHttp(request) { response in
    if response.success {
        showMainScreen()
    } else {
        showFailedLogin()
    }
}
```

Regulate The Access To The Code:

As a new beginner, it is important to adopt the culture of using the right control modifiers so that you can encapsulate your code. If you have the correct code encapsulation, it will play a big role in understanding the various pieces of the code which we write and engage with. All this will be possible without the need to recall out thought process.

Swift language has with it popular access control means such as the internal, private and public. However, the protected access is not present in the access control modifier of the Swift language. The reason for the absence lies in the fact that a subclass has the ability to expose a method which is protected using the new public method. Furthermore, the protected method will not provide extra optimization chances for the Swift compiler especially when we have a random new override emerging. The last reason is that protected modifier will contribute to a poor code encapsulation since it stops the subclass helpers from getting access to information available to the subclass.

Play Around With The Playgrounds:

A playground is one of the best places for new Swift developers. Here, you can try and build playgrounds which can help you do some testing and validation, share some concepts and validate the ideas with another. This can be achieved without heading to build a new project. If you would like to start a playground, you need to select it on the XCode launch.

Once you are on the playground, you should begin to code and see the results shown on the right.

You should take advantage of playgrounds and develop prototypes in Swift language.

Make Use Of The Optional In The Right Manner:

We say a property is optional if it has a valid or nil value. It is possible to unwrap an optional by adhering to the optional name using an exclamation point. This should be similar to the optionalProperty! This is something which you don't want to encounter.

However, we have certain cases where the application of the implicitly unwrapped optional is allowed. IBOutletsis an example. The outlets are optional since IBOoutLets are declared at a specific point after the initialization, and all the non-optional features need to possess the initialization based on the rules of Swift.

The NSNumber should be left behind:

The Objective-C uses primitives for both the numbers as well as the Foundation Objective –C. Some of the Swift types to use in place of the NSNUmber include:

- Float
- Double
- Swift
- Int
- Bool

We can still apply the NSNumber in the conversions between several types in the Objective-C, but Swift provides the idiomatic style of converting values.

Tips On How You Should Not Develop Apps In IOS:

1. Don't Put Every File In The Root Folder

You should make use of folders to show groups in the XCode. This is just like in real life where you don't have all your utensils in one collection. Just try to be organized as this is the best way which you will end up building wonderful projects. You should be aware that in the XCode 9 folders are developed to take care of your groups.

2. Avoid having warning in your project

You should make it a practice to fix any type of warning which shows up in your project. It is a bad practice to have warnings remain in your project. Although warnings exist, that should not be the reason for you to leave them in your project. If you want to be a bit radical, you should play around with the build flag which will help you kill warnings.

3. Your source code should not be very long

It is always annoying when you open a source file, and get greeted with a long source code which will make you scroll and scroll before you reach the end. You should adopt the SwiftLint which can trigger a warning so that you can remain aware whenever your code starts to become big.

4. Don't write a lot of code which you might never use

Don't make this mistakes of returning something inside the if else block. Instead, apply this style when you want to return something:

```
if something {
    return true
}
return false
```

The next thing you should notice about this tip is that you need to develop the right knowledge about how Swift functions operate. Don't just copy and paste, try to do some little modification. You should take time to think about the problem you want to solve and avoid copying the same code in many places. Just get time and create new functions and use them in the right manner.

5. Reinventing the when might cost you

If you find the right and best practice, then use it. However, at all times it is good to do some research online about the problem before you can start to code. Don't forget that there are a lot of people who experience the coding problem. Most of the time, you will find someone who had a similar issue like the one you would like to solve. A visit to the StackOverflow can save your time and day. Make use of the advantage of a community. Don't be shy to ask questions on the internet.

6. Connecting third party libs manually is wrong

You make a habit to use dependency managers such as Swift Package Manager. Do not add dependencies manually. It looks ugly.

7. Minimize on the number of dependencies

If you find a native solution go with that. But, do not use too many dependencies. One way to avoid excessive use of dependencies is by only using dependencies for tasks which are complex.

8. Don't write async code if you don't have operations, promises and third party libs

In Swift programming, you will write async code. So, before you end up messing up things, you need to make use of promises because they are an extensive abstraction over the async tasks. They simplify your life so that you have an easy life.

9. Don't use the Singletons

They are the cause of all evils. You should put a stop to Singletons if you are a fun of using them. If you are not sure how you can stop using them, do some deep research on the internet.

Conclusion

This book has been written to both macOS and IOS developers. Regardless of whether it is your first time to learn how to code or you are an experienced developer, there is something to learn here. If you are just getting started in Swift development, this book should be able to help you master the fundamentals in Swift programming.

The start of every journey in programming is to learn the language. For the IOS developers, this book starts the journey for you with the fundamentals of Swift programming language. This book generally prepares you to begin tackling complex stuff in the Swift language.

You should have realized that Swift language is not like the objective – C. Instead, it is much better and safe. Swift helps you get the best smart modern syntax. You have a language which is expressive and easy to understand. If you are done reading this book, the next step for you is to challenge yourself with even a complex Swift book. This will now help you grasp deep skills and concepts.

Practice to code every day, this book alone can't make you become an expert Swift developer. Perhaps you will need to put more effort into reading and writing code. Try several practical questions on building apps until when you feel confident of yourself. Remember, nothing comes on a silver platter. You have to dedicate your time and effort. We have done our part of helping you develop a basic understanding of Swift programming. Now, it is your chance to build and expand on that knowledge.

SWIFT

A Comprehensive Intermediate Guide to Learn and Master the Concept of Swift Programming

Introduction

Congratulations on purchasing *Swift: A Comprehensive Intermediate Guide to Learn and Master the Concept of Swift Programming* and thank you for doing so.

Swift is a powerful language that helps one to write great software. The software can be for desktops, servers, iPhones and anything else that can run the code. It is a language that is safe, fast and offers plenty of interaction. It combines the best features of a modern language and other great features from the open-source community. The Swift compiler is created to deliver quality performance. In addition, the language is optimized for development purposes.

Swift is a friendly language to new programmers. It is an industrial-quality programming language that is both enjoyable and expressive. If you write the Swift code in a playground, it gives you the opportunity to test the code and see the results instantly. This saves time of building and running an app. The language defines extensive classes of popular programming errors by borrowing modern programming patterns such as:

- Memory is controlled automatically

- Variables have to be initialized before they are used.

- Checking integers for overflow

- Error handling provides for recovery from unexpected issues

- Checking array indices for out-of-bounds errors

The swift code is compiled and effectively optimized so that it delivers the best performance. Both the syntax and standard library are created depending on the guiding principle of programming. This book provides you with the best lessons as an intermediate or advanced swift developer. The first chapter introduces you to how you can build adaptive user interfaces for your apps. In addition, you learn how to add sections and an index list in the UITableView. The remaining chapters teach you more concepts related to improving the design of your app. Finally, it concludes with how to get direction and draw routes on maps.

Chapter 1

Building Adaptive User Interface

The long story of Apple started with only one iPhone that had a 3.5-inch display. During this time, there was no big deal when it came to designing apps. In fact, you only required to account for two unique orientations. That is the portrait and orientation. After a few years, Apple created an iPad that had a 9.7-inch display. During this period, iOS developers created two different types of screen designs. One was for the iPhone and the other one was for the iPad.

Fast forward to 2018, you will agree that Apple has redefined its products. If you are a lover of Apple products, you must have seen a tremendous change in their devices. With the release of iPhone X, one can actually tell that this giant tech company has invested a lot in creating user-friendly products.

Right now, all iOS developers have a big challenge to develop generic apps that can adapt its User Interface in all Apple's devices and products. Moreover, this is part of Apple's goal to have apps that support any orientation and any iOS device display. Nowadays, apps adapt their UI to a given device and orientation.

This has resulted in a new UI design concept called Adaptive Layout. It started with the Xcode 7, this development tool lets developers create an app UI that can fit in all different devices, screen sizes, and orientation. When you look at the Xcode 8, the interface builder has been further re-defined and streamlined so that it can improve the adaptive user interface. In fact, it comes with a complete full live preview of how things can fit on any iOS device.

New techniques and ideas are involved when it comes to adaptive design. It consists of trait collections, size classes, adaptive fonts, auto layout, etc. Adaptive design helps developers to build universal and localized apps.

If you are an iOS developer, you must be aware of why adaptive design is that helpful. You know how difficult it is to auto-resize masks, keep track of orientations, and develop separate code paths depending on the type of device. Well, the adaptive design seeks to address all these issues.

Size Classes

To achieve an adaptive design, you must know how to use Size Classes. This is one of the most important things that make the adaptive layout a success. Size classes are an abstraction of the way a device is categorized based on the orientation and screen size. By using Size Classes, one is able to remove logic and code that addresses many different kinds of screen sizes, specific devices, and orientations. It further allows one to have a single interface for all devices.

Size Classes exist of two types, regular and compact. Each Size class can be represented both vertically and horizontally. Moreover, each device has its own Size Class, which includes all of its orientations. An iPad, for instance, is usually represented by a regular size class for its large screen.

Compact screen sizes, on the other hand, represent smaller screens, which mean less room. Devices in this size class would include iPhones and iPods. It may vary depending on orientation, however. See the table below:

	Vertically	Horizontally
iPhone Portrait	Regular	Compact
iPhone Landscape	Compact	Compact
iPhone 6 Plus Landscape	Compact	Regular
iPad Portrait	Regular	Regular
iPad Landscape	Regular	Regular

Step 1: Choose a Size Class in the Interface Builder

Proceed to Main.storyboard. The canvas will have a rectangular shape. The bottom of the interface will have "wAny hAny". This means "Any Width, Any Height." This means that anything that is changed on the canvas will affect all Size Classes. You may click on the button, which will show you that you can toggle several different classes.

Step 2: Add an Image

Click on an Image View from the Object Library and drag it towards the canvas. Using the Size Inspector, set the following attributes:

X Position = 0
Y Position = 72
Width = 600
Height = 218

Bring up the Attributes Inspector. Use it to modify the view's mode.

Step 3: Add a label

Bring up the Object Library. Find the label and drag it toward the canvas. Bring up the Size Inspector and set the following attributes:

X position = 16
Y position = 312
Width = 568
Height = 242

Afterwards, go to the Attributes Inspector. Make the following changes:

- Set Alignment to Center
- Set Text to "Silver Laptop"
- Modify the Font Size to System 100.0 points
- Set Lines to 0

Step 4: Adding Constraints

Let's add some constraints for the two objects we've just added.
Next, we want to add constraints for the label and image view. Go to the bottom of the Interface Builder and click Reset to Suggested Constraints located under All Views in View Controller part. In case you see the option greyed out, confirm that one of the views in the canvas is highlighted.

Step 5: Build and Run

At the top of the Xcode, click on iPad Retina so that you can use it for the IOS Simulator. Build and run the app by clicking Command + R. You will discover that the app does fine for the iPad. However, we need to make sure that it works well on any device.

Live Preview

To build and run your app so that you can tell how your user interface works can be tiresome. Fortunately, Xcode 6 has some added ability to allow live rendering of a user interface on any device in any particular orientation. This will allow one to resolve any auto layout problems faster than just running an app in the IOS Simulator every time.

Step 1: Enable Preview Assistant

Move to the top of the Xcode and click Assistant Editor button.
This will split the Xcode's editor into two panes. At the right pane, choose Automatic> Preview > Main.storyboard.

Step 2: Add devices to the Preview

Interface Builder will display a live preview of the user interface on a 4 inch iPhone. You will see that the user interface is less than the actual on the iPhone. If nothing shows up on the preview, click on the view controller located on the left pane to refresh it.

Navigate to the right pane, click the + button found at the bottom so that you can add more devices to the preview. Move on and add the iPad to the preview.

Step 3: Switch Orientations

In the assistant editor, hover your iPhone at the bottom. On the left of the device name, you will see a button, which switches the current orientation. Click it once so that you can switch the iPhone preview to the landscape orientation.

How to install Size Class and Specific Constraints

In case our user interface has some issues, we will require adding some constraints that are specific to a given size of a class. This is another benefit of using adaptive design. We are able to dictate to the user interface how it must lay out its views for specific size classes without adding another storyboard. Initially, it required one to use two different storyboards and load the right one during execution.

Step 1: Image View Base Constraints

First, add constraints that work for most devices and later improve them. Then, remove the constraints that had been added earlier. You do this by clicking any view in the canvas and then you select Editor > Resolve Auto Layout Issues > All Views in View Controller – Clear Constraints.

Choose the image view, click on the Align button, select Horizontal Center in the Container, and finally click Add 1 Constraint. You can then open the Size Inspector on the right and double-click to edit it.

Step 2: Add Label Base Constraints

As a result of the constraints added to the image view, the label already contains the height and vertical spacing from the image view added. Select the label and click the Pin button so that you can add a leading, vertical, and trailing space constraint. Next, if you preview the app in the assistant editor, the constraints make things much better. However, there's a challenge when the app uses a compact horizontal size class.

Step 3: Add a compact Horizontal constraint

Use the size class to toggle the button at the bottom, choose Compact Width, Compact Height. The bar will turn into a shade of blue to show that one is editing the user interface for a particular size class. Select the image view, open the Size Inspector, and update the frame. The next thing you should do is to open the label and update its frame in the Size Inspector.

While you have the label selected and the Size Inspector open, choose the label's constraints and remove it by pressing Delete. You can highlight multiple constraints by long pressing the Shift key. This will remove the constraints added for this Size Class.

Fortunately, Xcode has the ability to tell such constraints. It can either use the image view or selected label. Select Editor > Resolve Auto Layout Issues > All Views in View Controller – and then Reset to suggested Constraints.

Step 4: Preview Updated Constraints

You simply open the Size Inspector for the image view. You will find that there are different constraints listed but some that are greyed out and others aren't. This will show which constraints are active for the present size class.

Try to double-click on any one of them; the bottom part will reveal active classes and constraints.

Chapter 2

Add Section and Index List in the UITableView

An indexed table view represents a more or less plain-styled table view. The only execution is that it contains an index in the right side of the table view. The indexed table is very popular in iOS apps. The most popular examples include the built-in Contacts app on the iPhone. By delivering an index scrolling, users have a chance to access any given section in the table immediately without the need to go through every section.

Below are some of the methods that one will need to know if they want to add sections and index list to the UITableView.

- **NumberOfRowsInsection**: This method will show the total number of rows in a given section.

- **NumberOfSectionsInTableView:** This method shows the sum of sections contained in the table view. Most of the time the number is of the section is set to 1. In case you are interested in having multiple numbers, write a large number.

- **TitleForHeaderInSection**: This method will represent the header titles for different parts. It is an optional method in case you don't allocate section titles.

- **CellForRowAtIndexPath:** This one will return the table data for a given section.

- **SectionIndexTitlesForTableView:** This one returns the indexed titles that show up in the index list on the right side of the view.

- **SectionForSectionindexTitle.** This will display the index section that the table view has to jump when a user touches on a given index.

Demo App

This demo app is a simple app that will display a list of animals in the standard table view. However, this app will place the animals into various sections and offer a list of index list for rapid access. You can look at the image below to understand how the demo app will look.

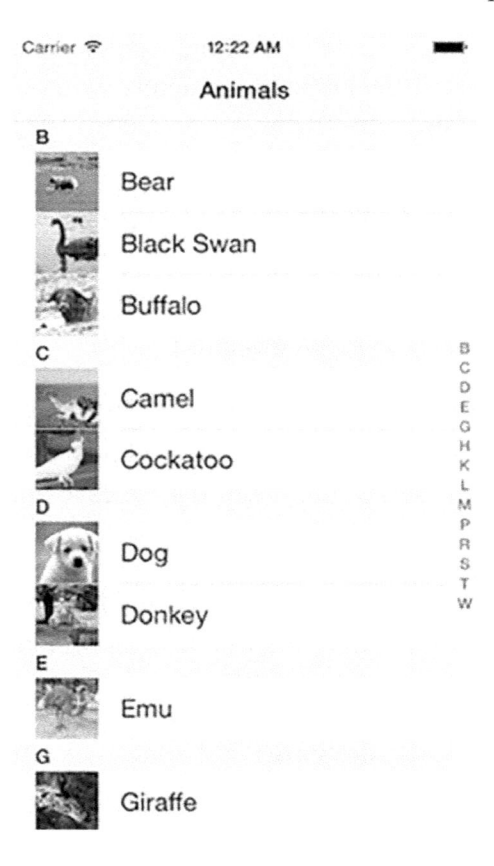

This chapter focuses on the implementation and index list. It is recommended that if you don't want to build the Xcode from scratch, download online the Xcode template.

How to display Sections in the UITableView

The animal data for this app is stored in the array. What is going to be done is that the data shall be organized into sections according to the alphabetical order. Since it is a demo app, you will replace the animal array with an NSDictionary. The first thing is to define and declare the animals' variable in the NSDictionary. Next, add another array for the section titles using the AnimalTableViewController.m.

```objc
@interface AnimalTableTableViewController () {
    NSDictionary *animals;
    NSArray *animalSectionTitles;
}
```

Navigate to the ViewDidLoad: method and alter the code. Change it into the following.

```objc
- (void)viewDidLoad
{
    [super viewDidLoad];

    animals = @{@"B" : @[@"Bear", @"Black Swan", @"Buffalo"],
                @"C" : @[@"Camel", @"Cockatoo"],
                @"D" : @[@"Dog", @"Donkey"],
                @"E" : @[@"Emu"],
                @"G" : @[@"Giraffe", @"Greater Rhea"],
                @"H" : @[@"Hippopotamus", @"Horse"],
                @"K" : @[@"Koala"],
                @"L" : @[@"Lion", @"Llama"],
                @"M" : @[@"Manatus", @"Meerkat"],
                @"P" : @[@"Panda", @"Peacock", @"Pig", @"Platypus", @"Polar Bear"],
                @"R" : @[@"Rhinoceros"],
                @"S" : @[@"Seagull"],
                @"T" : @[@"Tasmania Devil"],
                @"W" : @[@"Whale", @"Whale Shark", @"Wombat"]};

    animalSectionTitles = [[animals allKeys] sortedArrayUsingSelector:@selector(localizedCaseInsensitiveCompare:)];
}
```

In this code, the NSDictionary for the animal variable is created. The first letter of the animal is entered as a key. The value that relates with the associated key is the array of the animal names.

Furthermore, the *animalSectionTitles* array has been declared to store the section titles. For convenience purposes, use the keys of the animals in the dictionary to represent section titles. To retrieve the NSDictionary keys, one should call *allKeys: method*. In addition, the titles are sorted in alphabetical order.

The next thing is to modify the *numberOfSectionsInTableView: method* and display the sum of sections.

```
- (NSInteger)numberOfSectionsInTableView:(UITableView *)tableView
{
    // Return the number of sections.
    return [animalSectionTitles count];
}
```

To show the header title for every section, you must implement the *titleForHeaderInSection: method*. Return the section title according to the section index. The next thing is to let the table view understand the number of rows for a given section. Do this by creating the *numberOfRowsInSection: method* while in the AnimalTableViewController.m.

```
(NSInteger)tableView:(UITableView *)tableView numberOfRowsInSection:(NSInteger)section
{
    // Return the number of rows in the section.
    NSString *sectionTitle = [animalSectionTitles objectAtIndex:section];
    NSArray *sectionAnimals = [animals objectForKey:sectionTitle];
    return [sectionAnimals count];
}
```

Once the app begins the rendering process in the table view, the numberOfRowsInSection is called and a new section appears. Depending on the index of the section, one will get the section title and use it as a key to extract the animal names for the section and return the sum of the animal names for a given section. The last thing is to alter the *cellRowAtindexPath: method* as shown below:

```
- (UITableViewCell *)tableView:(UITableView *)tableView cellForRowAtIndexPath:(NSIndexPath *)indexPath
{
    UITableViewCell *cell = [tableView dequeueReusableCellWithIdentifier:@"Cell" forIndexPath:indexPath];

    // Configure the cell...
    NSString *sectionTitle = [animalSectionTitles objectAtIndex:indexPath.section];
    NSArray *sectionAnimals = [animals objectForKey:sectionTitle];
    NSString *animal = [sectionAnimals objectAtIndex:indexPath.row];
    cell.textLabel.text = animal;
    cell.imageView.image = [UIImage imageNamed:[self getImageFilename:animal]];

    return cell;
}
```

The index path has the current number of the row plus the current index section. Still, depending on the section index, it is possible to extract the section title and apply it as the key to highlight the animal names for a given section. Once you have done that you can hit the run button to see the result of the app.

If you want to add an index list to a table, you simply need to use a few lines of code. First, add the *sectionIndexTitlesForTableViw: Method* and display an array containing a section index. The section title is used as an index as shown below:

```
- (NSArray *)sectionIndexTitlesForTableView:(UITableView *)tableView
{
    return animalSectionTitles;
}
```

Once you do this you will be done. Try to run the app and see. You should see the index appear on the right side of the table. Surprisingly, no need of implementation and the indexing is fine. Tap any index and you will see a given section of the table.

In case you are working on a large project that you may need to show an extensive record, it will be better to arrange the data into different sections and offer an index list for quick access. This chapter has taught you how to implement the indexed table. So far, you must know how to add sections and index list in a table view using Swift language.

Chapter 3

Creating Simple View Animations in Swift

When Apple released iOS 7 and iOS 8, both animation and motion effects turned to be the focus of design both in Apple and other developers of Apple devices. The iOS 7 creates a flat and minimal design to apps. This led to certain apps sharing same UI. To create a difference from other apps, developers use motion effects and animations.

Animations don't just create a unique app but it improves the overall user experience in the application. If you want to see how animations enhance the UX, look at the Apple apps. The Photos app is a great example. If you select a photo from the collection, the photo will expand out and when you close it, it shrinks back to the original photo selected. This further improves the navigation of the app because it will allow a person to know exactly tell where they are if they browsed a collection of photos.

The Facebook's Paper app uses the same animation in a beautiful way to improve the general user experience. In this app, an article is selected by flipping it up. The article will expand out from its thumbnail version, meaning that if you flip the article downwards, it will return to its initial state. In this case, the animation is used to demonstrate how the app operates. If you were interacting with the app for the first time, you would still be able to figure out how to use it without any assistance.

Animations are a great thing. Apart from improving the user experience, animations make users want to continue using the app instead of uninstalling and searching for a better one in the App Store.

There are many different ways of adopting animation in apps. Some of those methods include using a UIKit Dynamic, View controller translations, and layer animations. This chapter examines simple view animations.

This chapter starts with a brief introduction of APIs applied in animating views. In addition, it will present examples of how one can use APIs in the app.

The Basic View Animations

For one to develop animations on views, he or she must change properties on views and allow UIKit to animate it automatically. The properties to change are marked Animatable. The list below shows properties that should be Animatable.

- Bounds
- Alpha
- Transform
- BackgroundColor
- Center
- ContentStretch

All animations include changing one or more of these properties.

When it comes to simple view animations, the UIKit has the following APIs to animate the views on the screen.

- UIView.animateWithDuration(_:,animations:,completion:)
- UIView.animateWithDuration(_:, delay:, options:, animations:, completion:)
- UIView.animateWithDuration(_:, animations:)

The last one accepts two parameters. The first value represents the duration of the animation in seconds and the properties that you want to change. The UIKit accepts the original state of the view and develops a smooth transition from one state to the next based on what one describes in the animation.

The remaining APIs aren't different from the last one but they accept additional parameters that create more configuration to the animation. The first one has a complete closure that one can use to describe another animation which you may want to happen after the first one or perform a cleanup of the UI.

The second API has two additional parameters. That is the delay and options. Delay represents the time one has to wait before the animation begins while UIViewAnimationOptions constant should show how one wants to carry out the animations.

Spring Animations

It models the attributes of a real-life spring. This means that when a view is moved from one point to another, it will shift to the end before finding a position. The method used for spring animations is shown below.

```
UIView.animateWithDuration(_:, delay:,
usingSpringWithDamping:, initialSpringVelocity:,
options:, animations:, completion:)
```

This method resembles the previous method with only two differences.

- The Spring with Damping
- Initial Spring Velocity

Damping refers to a value from 0 to 1 which determines how the view can return to the end of the animation. The near to 1 the value is, the less bouncy it can turn out to be. An initialSpringVelocity determines the initial velocity of the animation. This defines the starting strength of the animation. If you would like it to begin rapidly, then you have to set a large value. However, if you want a smooth animation, then you should set the value to 0.

Keyframe Animations

This will allow anyone to set different stages of the animation. One can group several animations together so that they can share common features but be able to control it individually.

The Keyframe animation APIs is as follows:

- UIView.addKeyframeWithRelativeStartTime(_:,relativeDuration:)
- UIView.animateKeyframesWithDuration(_:,delay:,options:,animations:)

These two methods are used as one with the first one nested in the first animations closure.

The first method will set the general configuration of the animation such as the period it should take, the delay and other options. One can then set one or more of the second method within the animations closure to prepare for the different stages of the animation.

The relative time of start and duration of each frame is a value which ranges between 0 and 1. This value represents the percentage of time in the total duration of the animation.

View Transitions

These transitions are important when you want to add a new view to your view or remove a view from the view hierarchy.

Important APIs that will help you create these view transitions include:

```
UIView.transitionWithView(_:, duration:, options:, animations:, completion:)
UIView.transitionFromView(_:, toView:, duration:, options:, completion:)
```

Use the first view transition to see the view hierarchy. This method accepts parameters the same as the previous animation methods.

The second method helps one to select a view from the view hierarchy and add a new view to its place.

Example

To get started, look for a reference of the constraints that can change. Open the storyboard file and select the constraints.

Chapter 4

JSON and Codable

Codable is one of those great protocols for Swift+. One can use it to encode and decode data formats. For example, JSON to native objects. It is possible for one to map Swift objects to JSON data just by using Codable protocol.

As an iOS developer, you are going to interact with JSON at one point in your life. Every web service right from Facebook to Foursquare uses JSON to fetch data for your app. The question is how can you effectively transform that JSON data into Swift objects?

In this Chapter, you will learn how to work with JSON objects in the Swift language with the help of the Codable protocol. This chapter will further extend into JSONEncoder and JSONDecoder. You will also learn how you can map between JSON and Swift structs.

Importance of Coding and Decoding

Well, what are some of the issues that Codable addresses? Let's study an example.

Assume you are creating a recipe app. This app will display a different list of recipe including instructions, ingredients, and basic information related to food. You receive data associated to the app from the web service as well as their API. This API has the JSON data format.

In brief, JSON is a text-based data format that has many web services including Foursquare, Facebook, and Twitter. Below is an example:

```
{
    "name": "Spaghetti Bolognese",
    "author": "Reinder's Cooking Corner",
    "url": "https://cookingcorner.com/spaghetti-bolognese",
    "yield": 4,
    "ingredients": ["cheese", "love", "spaghetti", "beef", "tomatoes", "garlic"],
    "instructions": "Cook spaghetti, fry beef and garlic, add tomatoes, add love, eat!"
}
```

JSON objects stay inside these brackets {}. Arrays stay inside square brackets [] while property names and strings remain inside quotes. Values can either be strings, arrays, numbers, and objects. However, this is not just interesting; the most interesting thing is that JSON is a great way for one to connect apps and web services.

You see, one of the great things about the internet is the way one can connect many computers in a network. Most of these computers communicate with one another using different protocols such as TCP, SSH, and HTTP. Many of these protocols depend on mutual agreements. The computers can communicate because there is a common language understood by each other.

Websites are created on top of these protocols. When a browser asks for this webpage from the web server, it receives a response that has the HTML format. In this case, the HTML describes the webpage, and then the browser renders it. Once this is done, anyone is able to see and read the page.

So, what has that to do with JSON? This is a format agreed on web services, apps, and APIs. All web apps and online services use it because the format is flexible and simple.

JSON has an amazing capability for one to encode any data format for web services, apps, and APIs. It is used in all online services, web apps because of the simple and flexible format.

JSON has one important ability: one can encode whichever data format in JSON as well as decode it back to any data format. It is this process of decoding and encoding that makes JSON very powerful.

Other data formats such as XML can still be encoded and decoded. JSON is a very popular format for apps and web services. One can select Swift Int, URL, Data, Double and Dictionary values then encode them into JSON. Then send them to the web service that decodes the values into a native format that understands it. Conversely, the web server transfers data encoded as JSON to an app as well as decode the data to native types such as Array and String.

Once the recipe app receives JSON, it's now possible to decode it into Swift struct as shown below:

```swift
struct Recipe {
    var name:String
    var author:String
    var url:URL
    var yield:Int
    var ingredients:[String]
    var instructions:String
}
```

Well, Codable becomes important is the time of encoding and decoding data from native types to different formats. Let's move on and see how it is done!

The Codable Protocol

Previously, to use JSON before Swift 4 was very difficult. One had to serialize the JSON and typecast each property of the JSON to the right Swift type. For example:

```swift
let json = try? JSONSerialization.jsonObject(with: data, options: [])

if let recipe = json as? [String: Any] {
    if let yield = recipe["yield"] as? Int {
        recipeObject.yield = yield
    }
}
```

It's hard to deal with possible errors and type discrepancies. While it might work, it's not the right one.

Libraries such as SwiftyJSON simplify the way one works with JSON but one will still require mapping the JSON data into its correct Swift properties and objecting.

However, Swift 4 allows one to use Codable protocol. That means that your Swift class and struct will have to use that protocol, and then you will find JSON encoding and decoding for free.

The Codable protocol consists of two protocols, Encodable and Decodable. Both of these protocols are minimal and seem to define the functions init(from: Decoder) and encode(to: Encoder).

In truth, the JSONDecoder class has code to convert the JSON format into a key-value container so that one can create their own encoder and decoder for any given format. Let's study an example. The first thing is to create a struct called User by doing this way:

```
struct User:Codable {
    var first_name:String
    var last_name:String
    var country:String
}
```

The User struct contains three simple properties of the type String and relates to the Codable protocol. Next, it is to write some bit of JSON. This is the JSON that we shall work with.

JSON data generally enters the app as the response of the web service request. However, in this example the JSON is kept in the JSON string like this:

```
let jsonString = """
{
    "first_name": "John",
    "last_name": "Doe",
    "country": "United Kingdom"
}
"""
```

The next thing to do is to decode the JSON and turn that into a User object. This is how it will look:

- The first thing is to change the JSON string into a Data object by calling the data (String:) function on the string. This is an important step.

- Next is to create the JSONDecoder object and call the decode (_: from:) function on it. This changes the JSON data into an Object of type User through decoding the JSON.

- The next thing is to print the last name of the user using print(user.last_name).

Sounds easy? Basically, you have mapped the JSON object into a Swift struct and decoded the JSON format into a native object that Swift can work with.

Decode with JSON Codable

Let's use the previous example and expand it. This is the JSON to use:

```
let jsonString = """
{
    "first_name": "John",
    "last_name": "Doe",
    "country": "United Kingdom"
}
"""
```

This has to be turned into a Data object.

This step is important. Rather than representing the JSON as a string, the JSON is stored as a native Data object. Look into this code and you will realize that it uses force unwrapping to work with the optional return value from data (using:). Next, unwrap the optional more elegantly!

Using this code above, one can respond to errors in case the data (using:) returns nil. One can as well apply the shown error message, or even allow the task to fail and save the diagnostic information in the log.

The next thing is to create a new JSONDecoder object.

Then use this decoder to decode the JSON data.

But the decode (_: from:) function can throw errors. This code will crash when that takes place. Then we can respond to any errors that arise using the code below:

```
do {
    let user = try decoder.decode(User.self, from: jsonData)
    print(user.last_name)
} catch {
    print(error.localizedDescription)
}
```

Therefore, the whole code will appear this way. This is how it's different.

The most important thing here is to avoid silencing errors. Just catch the error and respond to it using UX or UI by logging, retrying and fixing the task.

In case the JSON properties such as first_name is not the same with the Swift struct properties, CodingKeys becomes more important.

Each struct and class that is associated with Codable can define a special nested enumeration referred to as CodingKeys. Use it to declare the properties that need to be encoded and decoded plus their names. The

User struct in the example below has the property names changed from snake_case to CamelCase.

```swift
struct User:Codable
{
    var firstName:String
    var lastName:String
    var country:String

    enum CodingKeys: String, CodingKey {
        case firstName = "first_name"
        case lastName = "last_name"
        case country
    }
}
```

If you use this struct together with the previous examples, you will discover that one can use the User object with the new property names.

The CodingKeys is simple to explain. What it does is to map the properties and use the string values to pick the correct property names in the JSON data.

Encode Objects with JSON Codable

Is it possible to encode objects with JSON? Yes. It is done as shown below:

```swift
var user = User()
user.firstName = "Bob"
user.lastName = "and Alice"
user.country = "Cryptoland"

let jsonData = try! JSONEncoder().encode(user)
let jsonString = String(data: jsonData, encoding: .utf8)!
print(jsonString)
```

This is the output of the above code:

```
{"country":"Cryptoland","first_name":"Bob","last_name":"and Alice"}
```

What is going on here?

- The first thing is to define a User object and assign certain values to its properties.

- Next is to use encode (_:) to encode the user objects to a JSON Data object.

- The next thing is to convert the Data object into a String and print it out.

Examine carefully and you will realize that encoding has adhered to the above rules. Still, this example can be expanded so that one can deal with errors.

In this example, the output formatting property is used to encode the "pretty print" in the JSON data. This will create spaces, newlines, and tabs to help make the JSON string easy to read.

Chapter 5

Get Social with Swift

Applying social media features in our apps is not that way easy. Both Apple and Facebook introduced social network capability features, talk of iOS 5 and iOS 6. Before the introduction of these features, developers were required to add a full Facebook and Twitter SDK to facilitate sharing in the apps. Now that it's built in, it is very easy to combine these social features into an app.

To use Social Framework, it facilitates applications to network with other social media from just a single API without the need to handle authentication. Users can log in both to Twitter and Facebook at the OS level in the "Settings" app. This means that a developer doesn't need to go and integrate complete Twitter SDK or Facebook. Everything has been done for you already. It contains a system that provides a view controller for creating posts and an abstraction that permits the use of each social network's API over the HTTP. The Social network framework is a great framework because it offers an interface to network with other social media. With this particular framework, one has to just write a few lines of code to help show up the composer. Then users have an opportunity to publish or tweet a Facebook post on the app.

The social framework has an accessible class called *SLComposeViewController*. This class presents the standard view controller for users to create a tweet and Facebook post. It also permits developers to attach images, preset initial text as well as add URL to the post. When you want to create a simple sharing property, it is the only class that you require.

Let's get started.

The initial Setup

Navigate to the Xcode and click on create a new application. Then click on *SingleViewApplication.*

The next thing is to name the application.

Import Framework

Next, move to the framework section in the Xcode and add another Social Framework to the application. You can check in the image below.

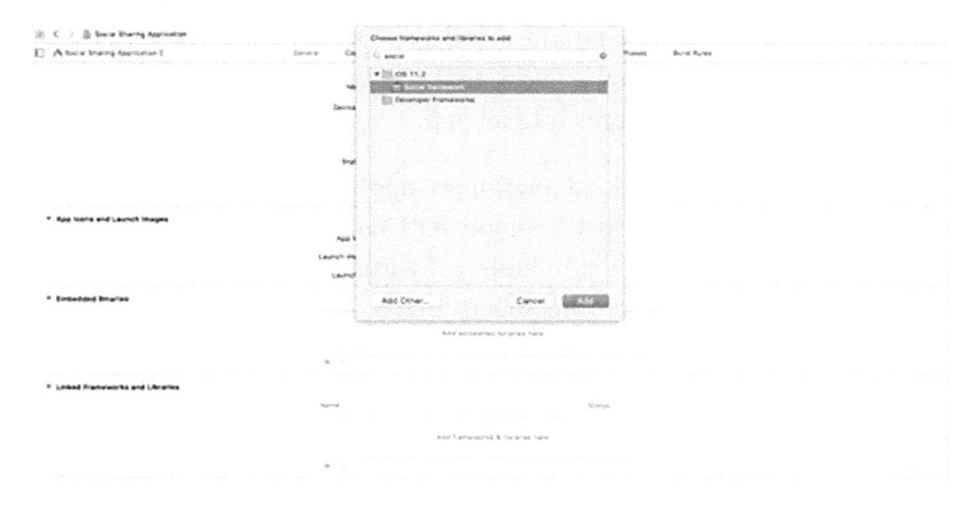

Interface Design

The next thing is to navigate to the interface of the application, where there is a need to add some objects to the view controller. However, the first thing is to create a view.

Below are the instructions to follow.

Move to File> New> Cocoa Touch Class>UIViewController

Name this view controller file as the *SocialViewController*. This is shown in the screenshot below.

Connect the view controller file with the view that will be important in the design and functionality.

Create a connection between variables and Elements

Next is to add some objects to the view controller.

1. The UIView. This will add a custom color to the view. In this example, the Hexa color is used.
2. UILablel. This label helps one write a text so that the design can look elegant.
3. UIButtons. Two buttons will be used so that more actions can be added to it later on.

If you follow everything outlined above. The image below shows how the view will appear.

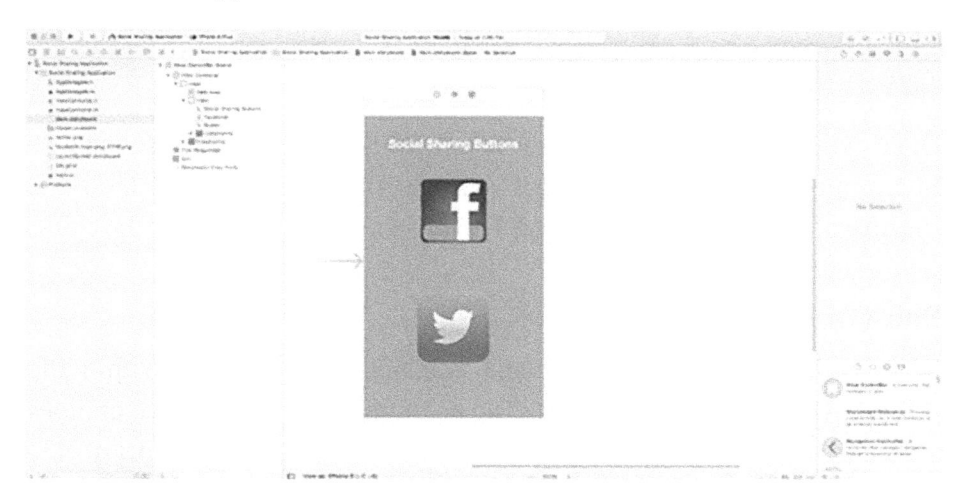

In this image, there are two images added.

To create a link between the objects and view, one has to perform a drag and drop of all objects one by one in the view controller.h file.

- Drag the first Facebook button and create an action using it.
- The next thing is to drag the second Twitter button and create its action. This has been shown below:

```
#import <UIKit/UIKit.h>

@interface SocialViewController : UIViewController

- (IBAction)facebookButton:(UIButton *)sender;

- (IBAction)twitterButton:(UIButton *)sender;

@end
```

Add Facebook Support

In this section, functionality is added to the Facebook sharing feature of the iOS application by using the help of a social framework. The next thing is to add a social framework to the view controller file.

```
#import <Social/Social.h>
```

Once you have done this the next thing is to make use of the SLComposeViewController class and add the view that will facilitate sharing of social media update on Facebook.

Point to note

Make sure that your social media account is configured within the iPhone settings and in case there is no account, there shall be two choices with a custom alert to select cancel or select the settings option.

Twitter Support

This section will illustrate how you can add Twitter functionality and share your social media update by using the twitter button.

Twitter is among the top ways for one to share their feeling and some tweet using twitter. The iOS offers Twitter support by providing the SocialFramework.

1. **First Step**

The first thing is to add the code into the twitter button and use its action to share our tweet on the twitter profile.

Make sure that you first add your personal Twitter details into the Twitter setting within your iPhone. By doing this it will not keep asking you to add the account to it.

2. **Second step**

Add the code below that makes active the function of the twitter button.

```
(IBAction)twitterButton:(UIButton *)sender {
    SLComposeViewController *tweetSheet = [SLComposeViewController composeViewControllerForServiceType:SLServiceTypeTwitter];
    [tweetSheet setCompletionHandler:^(SLComposeViewControllerResult result) {
        switch (result) {
            case SLComposeViewControllerResultCancelled:
            {
                NSLog(@"Post Failed");
                UIAlertController* alert;
                alert = [UIAlertController alertControllerWithTitle:@"failed!!" message:@"Something went wrong while sharing on Twitter, Please try again later." preferredStyle:UIAlertControllerStyleAlert];
                UIAlertAction* defaultAction = [UIAlertAction actionWithTitle:@"Okay" style:UIAlertActionStyleDefault handler:^(UIAlertAction * action) {

                }];
```

```
                [alert addAction:defaultAction];
                dispatch_async(dispatch_get_main_queue(), ^{
                    [self presentViewController:alert animated:YES completion:nil];
                });

                break;
            }
            case SLComposeViewControllerResultDone:
            {
                NSLog(@"Post Sucessful");
                UIAlertController* alert;
                alert = [UIAlertController alertControllerWithTitle:@"Success" message:@"Your post has been successfully shared." preferredStyle:UIAlertControllerStyleAlert];
                UIAlertAction* defaultAction = [UIAlertAction actionWithTitle:@"Okay" style:UIAlertActionStyleDefault handler:^(UIAlertAction * action) {}];
```

```
        [alert addAction:defaultAction];
        dispatch_async(dispatch_get_main_queue(), ^{
            [self presentViewController:alert animated:YES completion:nil];
        });
        break;
    }
    default:
        break;
    }
}];
[self presentViewController:tweetSheet animated:YES completion:Nil];
}
```

This will work in the same way a Facebook code operates. It will display success or failure status when updating the status.

Add image to the post

When you want the post to have an image. The process is quite simple. All you require to do is to write a single line of code and leave the rest to be done independently.

This will use the tweet sheet image sharing the property that one can use to add the custom image inside it.

By using this code, it will help a developer to add an image to the post. Don't forget to add an image to the asset folder before you can call it using this code.

For those who don't know how they can create a custom alert of their choice. You can use the method below. The alert view is outdated and in its place, there is going to be an alert controller that has the updated code in regard to the Apple's guidelines.

The first thing is to create an alert controller object and link the message, title and alert type to it. The next thing is to add an alert action that can perform an action once a user clicks on any given object action. Lastly, add the action inside the alert controller object and display the view using the presentViewController method.

If you follow each step outlined here, you will have created an application that can help you share your social status on the social media networks without going to use API. Nowadays, it is very easy to integrate Twitter and Facebook when you choose to use Social Framework in iOS 6. In case, you are creating an app, there is every reason why you should use it. It will add value to your app and boost your popularity.

```
public func font(forTextStyle textStyle: UIFont.TextStyle) -> UIFont {
    guard let fontDescription = styleDictionary?[textStyle.rawValue],
        let font = UIFont(name: fontDescription.fontName, size: fontDescription.fontSize) else {
            return UIFont.preferredFont(forTextStyle: textStyle)
    }

    let fontMetrics = UIFontMetrics(forTextStyle: textStyle)
    return fontMetrics.scaledFont(for: font)
}
```

To use it with the *Noteworthy.plist*, load it in the controller:

Chapter 6

Send SMS AND MMS in Swift language

The Message UI framework is not designed for email purposes but it also delivers specialized view controller for developers to submit a standard interface to compose SMS text message in the apps. While one uses the MFMailComposeViewController class for the email. This same framework facilitates MFMessageComposeViewController to deal with a text message.

Generally, how the MFMessageComposeViewController is applied is the same as the mail composer class. Don't worry because this section will go through the MFMessageComposeViewController class so that you can understand how to use it.

A demo app

This app will show a list of files in a table format. However, rather than presenting the main composer, the app will display a message on the interface with a pre-populated message content any time a user touches on any table rows.

Let's get started

To save time from the need to create the Xcode project, get a template to start to code. However, a new programmer of iOS SDK, you are advised to create the project from scratch. There are various programming tutorials that one can depend on to learn more from the table view as well as the storyboard.

Import Message UI Framework

The first thing to do is to import the MessageUI framework into the project.

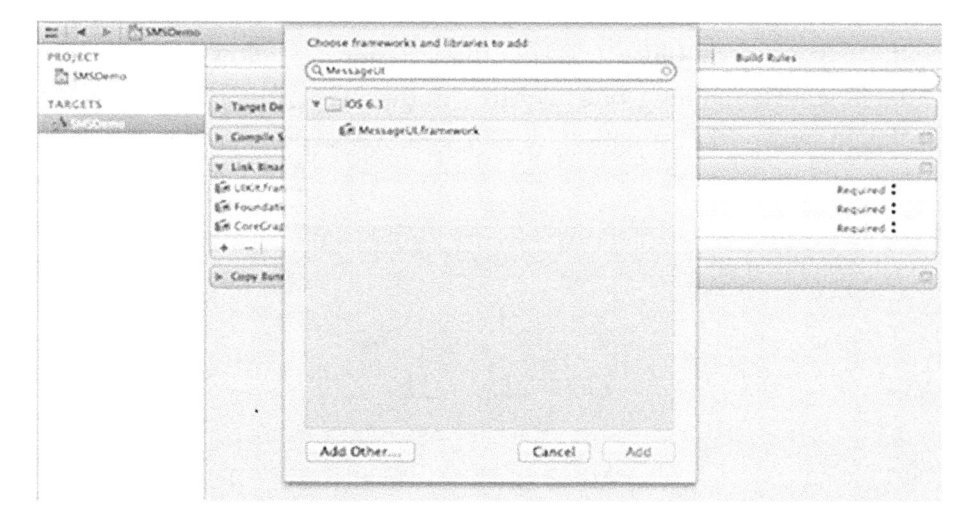

How to implement the Delegate?

Navigate to the "AttachmentTableViewController.m" then add the code below to the import MessageUI header and implement the MFMessageComposeViewControllerDelagate.

```
#import <MessageUI/MessageUI.h>

@interface AttachmentTableViewController () <
MFMessageComposeViewControllerDelegate>
```

The MFMessageComposeViewControllerDelagate protocol declares a single method that can be called anytime a user completes composing an SMS message. There is a need to deliver the implementation method that can deal with different situations.

1. The user cancels SMS editing.

2. The user touches on the send button and the SMS is sent and delivered successfully.

3. The user touches on the send button but there is no SMS send.

Next, you should add the code below to the "AttachmentTableViewController.m". In this stage, an alert message is displayed when the situation 3 happens. Other cases, the message composer is dismissed.

```
(void)messageComposeViewController:(MFMessageComposeViewController *)controller didFinishWithResult:(MessageComposeResult)result
{
    switch (result) {
        case MessageComposeResultCancelled:
            break;
        case MessageComposeResultFailed:
        {
            UIAlertView *warningAlert = [[UIAlertView alloc] initWithTitle:@"Error" message:@"Failed to send SMS!" delegate:nil cancelButtonTitle:@"OK" otherButtonTitles:nil];
            [warningAlert show];
            break;
        }
        case MessageComposeResultSent:
            break;
        default:
            break;
    }
    [self dismissViewControllerAnimated:YES completion:nil];
}
```

Creating the Message Composer

If a user clicks on any of the rows, the selected file is retrieved and call a custom method to show up the message composer. Update the "didSelectRowAtindexPath:" method using the code below:

```
- (void)tableView:(UITableView *)tableView didSelectRowAtIndexPath:(NSIndexPath *)indexPath
{
    NSString *selectedFile = [_files objectAtIndex:indexPath.row];
    [self showSMS:selectedFile];
}
```

The key method here is the "showSMS:" method that initializes and populates the default content of the SMS text message. Add the code below:

```
(void)showSMS:(NSString*)file {

    if(![MFMessageComposeViewController canSendText]) {
        UIAlertView *warningAlert = [[UIAlertView alloc] initWithTitle:@"Error" message:@"Your device doesn't support SMS!"
            delegate:nil cancelButtonTitle:@"OK" otherButtonTitles:nil];
        [warningAlert show];
        return;
    }

    NSArray *recipients = @[@"12345678", @"72345524"];
    NSString *message = [NSString stringWithFormat:@"Just sent the %@ file to your email. Please check!", file];

    MFMessageComposeViewController *messageController = [[MFMessageComposeViewController alloc] init];
    messageController.messageComposeDelegate = self;
    [messageController setRecipients:recipients];
    [messageController setBody:message];

    // Present message view controller on screen
    [self presentViewController:messageController animated:YES completion:nil];
}
```

Although many of the iOS devices should have the ability to send a text message, being a programmer you have the role to facilitate an exception. Assume if the app is used with an iPod touch that has the iMessage disabled. In such a situation, one can be sure that the device cannot send a text message. Therefore, at the start of the code, the device has to be verified to make sure that it can send a text message using the "canSendText" method in the MFMessageComposeViewController.

The remaining code is easy to understand. One can pre-populate multiple recipients phone numbers in the text message. For instance, the message body allows only textual content alone.

When the content is ready, call the "presentModalViewController:" to show up the message to the composer.

Time to compile and run the app

Once you have done all these, you are good to go. It is time to run the app and see the results. However, make sure that you test the device on a real iOS device. A simulator cannot permit one to send SMS.

Suppose you don't prefer in-app SMS

The previous implementation delivers a seamless integration of the SMS feature in the app. But let's assume that you only want to redirect to the default Messages app and send a text message. It becomes more simple. You can achieve that in a single line of code.

```
[[UIApplication sharedApplication] openURL: @"sms:98765432"];
```

In the iOS, an individual is allowed to communicate with other apps with the help of the URL. The mobile OS comes with the built-in support of the HTTP, tel, mailto and SMS URL schemes. In case you open the HTTP URL, the default iOS launches the URL using Safari. If you are interested in opening the Messages app, use the SMS URL schedule and describe in detail the recipient. But these schemes of URL don't support one to show up the default content.

Chapter 7

Custom Fonts and Dynamic Type

Custom font and dynamic type took time and effort before it was scaled for each text style when a user changes the dynamic type size. Apple created a new font metrics class in iOS 11 that made it easy and simple. It reduced the pain that previously existed.

The Dynamic Type

This was introduced by Apple in the iOS 7 to present a user with a system-wide mechanism to convert the desired text size from the system settings. To facilitate the use of Dynamic type, one has to define labels, text views and text fields to a specific font presented by UIFont class method called preferred font(forTextStyle:). The font returned has the Apple San Francisco typeface. This contains both size and weight modified for the user's size preference and the desired text style. For instance, to build a label that has the body text style:

```
let label = UILabel()
label.font = UIFont.preferredFont(forTextStyle: .body)
label.adjustsFontForContentSizeCategory = true
```

Some notes

- Apple created the adjustsFontForContentSizeCategory property to UITextField, UILabel and UITextView in the iOS 10. If it is true, the font will automatically be updated when the user alters the required font size. In case of iOS 9 and other earlier versions, one should listen for the UIContentSizeCategoryDidChange notification and update the font manually.

- The iOS 10 also provides one with a font that is compatible with the size class using the preferred font (forTextStyle: compatibileWith:).

- There are six UIFontTextStyle values that have been introduced in the iOS 7(. subheadline, body,. caption1, .footnote, caption2). There are four more styles added by iOS 9 (. title1, title2, title3 and. callout). iOS 11 adds the large style title(. largeTitle).

Below, you can look at how the different styles appear at extra small, large and accessibility extra-extra-extra-large sizes.

Title 1	Title 1	**Title 1**
Title 2	Title 2	**Title 2**
Title 3	Title 3	**Title 3**
Headline	Headline	**Headline**
Subheadline	Subheadline	Subheadline
Body	Body	Body
Callout	Callout	Callout
Footnote	Footnote	Footnote
Caption 1	Caption 1	Caption 1
Caption 2	Caption 2	Caption 2

Pay attention in the way all the text styles increase in size with accessibility. This is a new feature in iOS 11. Remember. Larger accessibility sizes introduced in iOS 7 are applied to the body style alone.

Scale A Custom Font

Before the release of iOS 11 that supported the dynamic type using a custom font, an individual was supposed to change the details of the font for every ten text styles and determine how to scale the font choices for each of the twelve content size categories.

Apple releases the font metrics used for the San Francisco typeface in the iOS Human Interface Guidelines. This is an important starting point that helps one to decide how they can scale each text style.

For instance, the. headline text style has a Semi-bold face that has 17 pt with the large content size and 23 pt at the xxxLarge size.

Font Metrics

To simplify the processing of scaling a custom font for the dynamic type, Apple introduced the UIFontMetrics in the iOS 11. To make use of a custom font for a specific text style, one has to first get the font metrics for each style and use it to scale the custom font.

Let's go back to the example of setting a label to the body text style but using a custom font. The correct action to take is as follows:

```
let font = UIFont(name: fontName, size: fontSize)
let fontMetrics = UIFontMetrics(forTextStyle: .body)
label.font = fontMetrics.scaledFont(for: font)
```

The font is developed using a custom font face and size. Look for the font metrics of the. body style and apply the scaledFont(for:) to receive the font scaled of the preferred text size.

The UIFontMetrics class eliminates the need to have a table of fonts for every twelve content size category. Still, you require to choose on a font for every style at the default content size.

Style Dictionary

To prevent the scenario of scattered names and sizes through the code, this example has a style dictionary that contains the face name and size applied at each of the styles at the. large content size. To reduce the complexity of customization as well as changing the typefaces. The style dictionary has been kept in a plist file.

This is the way it appears in the Noteworthy typeface that Apple bundles using iOS. It contains both a bold and light face.

Key	Type	Value
▼ Root	Dictionary	(11 items)
▶ UICTFontTextStyleTitle0	Dictionary	(2 items)
▶ UICTFontTextStyleTitle1	Dictionary	(2 items)
▶ UICTFontTextStyleTitle2	Dictionary	(2 items)
▶ UICTFontTextStyleTitle3	Dictionary	(2 items)
▼ UICTFontTextStyleHeadline	Dictionary	(2 items)
fontName	String	Noteworthy-Bold
fontSize	Number	17
▶ UICTFontTextStyleSubhead	Dictionary	(2 items)
▼ UICTFontTextStyleBody	Dictionary	(2 items)
fontName	String	Noteworthy-Light
fontSize	Number	17
▶ UICTFontTextStyleCallout	Dictionary	(2 items)
▶ UICTFontTextStyleFootnote	Dictionary	(2 items)
▶ UICTFontTextStyleCaption1	Dictionary	(2 items)
▶ UICTFontTextStyleCaption2	Dictionary	(2 items)

In this example, the. large font size for apple text size has been used for every style. For example, a 17 pt Noteworthy-Bold of the. the headline and a 17 pt Noteworthy-Light for the. body.

To use the fonts, one has to wrap the dictionary into a ScaledFont utility class which one has to initialize with the name of the plist file. The font(forTextStyle:) method shows a scaled font for every style.

```swift
public final class ScaledFont {
    public init(fontName: String)
    public func font(forTextStyle textStyle: UIFontTextStyle) -> UIFont
}
```

Look at the code for the complete details but there is an interesting way which searches for the font for each text style and applies the UIFontMetrics to show the scaled font. In case the style dictionary does not contain an entry for the text style, it will use the Apple preferred font:

```swift
private let fontName = "Noteworthy"

private lazy var scaledFont: ScaledFont = {
    return ScaledFont(fontName: fontName)
}()
```

Then when you want to set the font for a label, you call the font(forTextStyle:)

```swift
let label = UILabel()
label.font = scaledFont.font(forTextStyle: textStyle)
label.adjustsFontForContentSizeCategory = true
```

When the font is scaled using UIFontMetrics, the property called adjustsFontForContentSizeCategory will continue to work. This means there will be no need to worry about updating when the user changes the size. This is how it will appear in the Noteworthy font.

Title 1
Title 2
Title 3
Headline
Subheadline
Body
Callout
Footnote
Caption 1
Caption 2

Title 1
Title 2
Title 3
Headline
Subheadline
Body
Callout
Footnote
Caption 1
Caption 2

Title 1

Title 2

Title 3

Headline

Subheadline

Body

Callout

Footnote

Caption 1

Caption 2

Custom Font

There are no restrictions to apply the typefaces in the iOS. Remember. This is NotoSans extracted from google fonts. It contains regular, italic, bold and bold-italic faces. The italic has been used both for the subheadline and caption styles.

Title 1	Title 1	**Title 1**
Title 2	Title 2	
Title 3	Title 3	**Title 2**
Headline	**Headline**	
Subheadline	*Subheadline*	**Title 3**
Body	Body	
Callout	Callout	**Headline**
Footnote	Footnote	
Caption 1	*Caption 1*	*Subheadline*
Caption 2	*Caption 2*	
		Body
		Callout
		Footnote
		Caption 1
		Caption 2

If you want to download and add custom font files into your project, it is important to remember to add them into the target and arrange them under the "Fonts provided by application" key in the Info.plist:

▼ Fonts provided by application	Array	(3 items)
Item 0	String	NotoSerif-Regular.ttf
Item 1	String	NotoSerif-Bold.ttf
Item 2	String	NotoSerif-Italic.ttf

If you are not sure which font names to apply, use the code below with all the variable names in the code snippet:

```
let families = UIFont.familyNames
families.sorted().forEach {
  print("\($0)")
  let names = UIFont.fontNames(forFamilyName: $0)
  print(names)
}
```

Override the iOS Dynamic Type font family

The recent releases of iOS allow Dynamic Type. This is a great system for one to add accessible typography in the app. Choosing to use a Dynamic Type lets the user define a system-wide font size that can then be reflected in the app. The Dynamic Type supports different predefined text styles such as footnotes, titles, and captions that one can use to change the typographical salience of the content.

This marketing approach makes it look great but one is left surprised why not every app supports it. But the Dynamic Type has a huge drawback. For one to make an app unique from the rest, one should use the custom fancy-pants font. However, this is not permitted by the Dynamic Type.

Modify Font Descriptors

By using the UIFontDescriptor class, one can get some type of specification for every font. The descriptor shall codify the information such as weight, font family, style and font name. To get a descriptor from a font is very easy: one basically selects it from the fontDescriptor property of the UIFont. To change the descriptor to the original font, you pass an argument to the UIFont constructors.

The target here is to pick a font instance build by Dynamic Type and change the font that has a custom family name but still maintains all the other properties. This is not easy because it can change the font family name of a descriptor. Therefore, the font is reset. In addition, if the font descriptor is selected and a few changes are done, the final outcome is a font descriptor that has some properties which override the custom font family in other occasions.

This requires one to be smart. The first thing is to extract the required font traits and create a new font descriptor from nothing and detail the precise traits that are required. This is shown in this code snippet:

```swift
// Get a font from Dynamic Type
var font = UIFont.preferredFont(forTextStyle: UIFontTextStyleHeadline)

// Our overridden font family name
let newFamilyName = "Avenir Next"

// Extract the weight
let weight = (font.fontDescriptor.object(forKey: UIFontDescriptorTraitsAttribute)
    as! NSDictionary)[UIFontWeightTrait]!

// Create a new font traits dictionary
let attributes = [
    UIFontDescriptorTraitsAttribute: [
        UIFontWeightTrait: weight
    ]
]

// Create a new font descriptor
let descriptor = UIFontDescriptor(name: font.fontName, size: font.pointSize)
    .withFamily(newFamilyName)
    .addingAttributes(attributes)

// Find a font that matches the descriptor
font = UIFont(descriptor: descriptor, size: font.pointSize)
```

The global font family overrides appearance proxy

The method presented above is still powerful and one is supposed to set the fonts manually everywhere. The code can be altered into a computed property that an individual can define globally using the UIAppearance proxy protocol. This is shown below:

```
{
    var fontFamily: String {
        get {
            // Extract the font family from the current descriptor. This is not really
            // necessary but provides a sane value for the required getter.
            return font.fontDescriptor.object(forKey: UIFontDescriptorFamilyAttribute)
                as! String
        }
        set {
            // Extract the weight
            let weight = (font.fontDescriptor.object(forKey: UIFontDescriptorTraitsAttribute)
                as! NSDictionary)[UIFontWeightTrait]!

            // Create a new font traits dictionary
            let attributes = [
                UIFontDescriptorTraitsAttribute: [
                    UIFontWeightTrait: weight
                ]
            ]

            // Create a new font descriptor
            let descriptor = UIFontDescriptor(name: font.fontName, size: font.pointSize)
                .withFamily(newValue)
                .addingAttributes(attributes)

            // Find and set a font that matches the descriptor
            font = UIFont(descriptor: descriptor, size: font.pointSize)
        }
    }
}
```

By using a single line of code, one can automatically override the font family of the UILabel instances in the app while still retaining the font style and size from the Dynamic Type. Simply add the line below into the application delegate class:

```
UILabel.appearance().fontFamily = "Avenir Next"
```

When you have this line, one can configure the labels to use a predefined Dynamic Type Class for the best accessibility as well as enjoy a typographical fanciness of a custom font.

Chapter 8

Create Better iOS Animations

Animations are important in creating a unique user experience. They serve various needs and purposes including catching the attention of the user and directing their actions to results on the screen.

Animations further develop a unique experience for the app user. Animations support a specific level of responsiveness and interaction that is not possible in other areas. To develop better animations, one is supposed to create a sense of connection between the user interaction and visual changes. One of the ways that you can achieve this is to develop complete interaction in animations.

The importance of Interactive Animations

Interactive animations existed from a long time ago since the release of the first iPhone. The first appearance of the original iPhone was the "slide to unlock" screen, in this version the user had to directly move the slider before he or she could unlock the device. This specific type of animation was intuitive to those that had never used a multi-touch device.

Interactive animations allow a user to have freedom over the user interface. A direct manipulation is one of the natural interaction models most importantly on mobile devices. It integrates the actions to on-screen animations and provides complete control over a cancellation of the actions.

Furthermore, it appears great, users are able to relate an app the way it looks and how better it works. Therefore, when it appears great, they will pardon other issues with the app. This chapter will guide you on how to create interactive popup animation using Swift language.

UIViewProprtyAnimator

This property was added to the UIKit in the iOS 10 and upgraded in the iOS 11. It delivers a UIView-level object-oriented API to build animations. If you use a traditional UIVIew animation, you will need to write something close to this:

```
UIView.animate(withDuration: 1, delay: 0, options: [.curveEaseOut], animations: {
    self.myView.transform = CGAffineTransform(translationX: 50, y: 0)
    self.myView.alpha = 0.5
}, completion: nil)
```

However, if you are to use the UIViewProprtyAnimator, this is how you are going to write.

```
let animator = UIViewPropertyAnimator(duration: 1, curve: .easeOut, animations: {
    self.myView.transform = CGAffineTransform(translationX: 50, y: 0)
    self.myView.alpha = 0.5
})
animator.startAnimations()
```

This code resembles the UIViewPropertyAnimator, first, you need to develop an animator object and call startAnimation() rather than call a static method on the UIView class.

UIViewPropertyAnimator is very useful when the animation increases in complexity. Before going to look at the code, it is necessary to study the state machine backing UIViewPropertyAnimator.

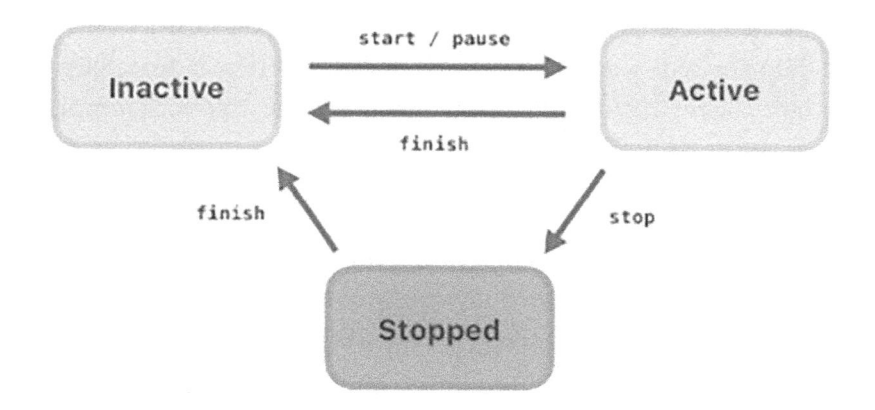

An animator can assume any of the above three possible states. That includes active, inactive and stopped. An animator is defined and initialized while in the inactive state but it will change to an active state when it is paused or started. Once the animation is complete, it goes back to the inactive state. When a started animation is paused, it continues to be in the active state and it can't go through a state transition.

Let's look at how you can apply the UIPanGestureRecognizer plus the UIViewPropertyAnimator to create an animation.

```
var animator = UIViewPropertyAnimator()
private func handlePan(recognizer: UIPanGestureRecognizer) {
    switch recognizer.state {
    case .began:
        animator = UIViewPropertyAnimator(duration: 3, curve: .easeOut, animations: {
            myView.transform = CGAffineTransform(translationX: 275, y: 0)
            myView.alpha = 0
        })
        animator.startAnimation()
        animator.pauseAnimation()
    case .changed:
        animator.fractionComplete = recognizer.translation(in: myView).x / 275
    case .ended:
        animator.continueAnimation(withTimingParameters: nil, durationFactor: 0)
    default:
        ()
    }
}
```

Please note that the pauseAnimation() has to be called instantly after the startAnimation(). Since this animation starts on a pan gesture, chances are that the user will want to scrub the animation first before they can release their touch. If the animation is paused, the fraction completed property is set to shift the view along with the user's touch.

Attempting to do this using the standard UIView animations, more logic will be required than what is shown in the above code snippet. The UIView animations don't have a simple way that one can directly take charge of the completion percentage of the animation or even permit one to pause and resume the animation to the end.

A popup Menu

This section shall teach you how to create a complete interactive, scrubbable, interruptible and reversible popup menu. There are 10 steps to follow. To make everything simple, all the views are created and modified in the code, even though this code can still operate with views build in the storyboard. Furthermore, the code will be inside the ViewController. Swift file.

1. Touch to open and close

The first thing is to make the popup view animate the states between open and close. No fancy additions are done here, simply use the basics of UIViewProperty Animator.

```swift
private enum State {
    case closed
    case open
}

extension State {
    var opposite: State {
        switch self {
        case .open: return .closed
        case .closed: return .open
        }
    }
}

class ViewController: UIViewController {

    private lazy var popupView: UIView = {
        let view = UIView()
        view.backgroundColor = .gray
        return view
    }()

    override func viewDidLoad() {
        super.viewDidLoad()
        layout()
        popupView.addGestureRecognizer(tapRecognizer)
    }
```

```swift
        transitionAnimator.addCompletion { position in
            switch position {
            case .start:
                self.currentState = state.opposite
            case .end:
                self.currentState = state
            case .current:
                ()
            }
            switch self.currentState {
            case .open:
                self.bottomConstraint.constant = 0
            case .closed:
                self.bottomConstraint.constant = 440
            }
        }
        transitionAnimator.startAnimation()
    }

}
```

```swift
private var bottomConstraint = NSLayoutConstraint()

private func layout() {
    popupView.translatesAutoresizingMaskIntoConstraints = false
    view.addSubview(popupView)
    popupView.leadingAnchor.constraint(equalTo: view.leadingAnchor).isActive = true
    popupView.trailingAnchor.constraint(equalTo: view.trailingAnchor).isActive = true
    bottomConstraint = popupView.bottomAnchor.constraint(equalTo: view.bottomAnchor, constant: 440)
    bottomConstraint.isActive = true
    popupView.heightAnchor.constraint(equalToConstant: 500).isActive = true
}

private var currentState: State = .closed

private lazy var tapRecognizer: UITapGestureRecognizer = {
    let recognizer = UITapGestureRecognizer()
    recognizer.addTarget(self, action: #selector(popupViewTapped(recognizer:)))
    return recognizer
}()

@objc private func popupViewTapped(recognizer: UITapGestureRecognizer) {
    let state = currentState.opposite
    let transitionAnimator = UIViewPropertyAnimator(duration: 1, dampingRatio: 1, animations: {
        switch state {
        case .open:
            self.bottomConstraint.constant = 0
        case .closed:
            self.bottomConstraint.constant = 440
        }
        self.view.layoutIfNeeded()
    })
}
```

The correct animation code is within the popupViewTapped function called after the view is tapped. So what one has to do is create an animator, assign animations to change the value of a constraint and begin the animator.

A state enum is introduced to show if the popup is closed or open. In addition, there is a computed opposite property that displays the opposite of the current state. This can also be implemented using a boolean flag, but it is very easy to reason about once the animation code turns complex.

One of the most important things to highlight is that the value of the constraint is manually getting updated when the animation ends. This has to be automatically done using the animator, however, if you could fix it explicitly then you could repair some edge-case bugs.

2. Adding a pan gesture

To make an animation interactive, there is a need to introduce a second gesture recognizer. This allows the user to begin and interrupt the animation by swiping over the popup view.

```
@objc private func popupViewPanned(recognizer: UIPanGestureRecognizer) {
    switch recognizer.state {
    case .began:
        animateTransitionIfNeeded(to: currentState.opposite, duration: 1.5)
        transitionAnimator.pauseAnimation()
    case .changed:
        let translation = recognizer.translation(in: popupView)
        var fraction = -translation.y / popupOffset
        if currentState == .open { fraction *= -1 }
        transitionAnimator.fractionComplete = fraction
    case .ended:
        transitionAnimator.continueAnimation(withTimingParameters: nil, durationFactor: 0)
    default:
        ()
    }
}
```

This code resembles the previous example with just one difference. This supports interruption of the animation. As you can see, the animation code has been refactored into a function called animateTransitionIfNeeded that drives the rest of the code that was initially inside the popuViewTapped function.

3. **Record the progress of the animation and fix the interruption offset**

A problem arises when an animation is interrupted, that is it shifts away from the user's touch. This is as a result of the panhandler not handling the current progress of the animation. To solve this problem, there is a need to record the fraction completed by the animator and use it as the baseline when one calculates a pan offset. A property will be required to record the current progress of the animation.

```
private var animationProgress: CGFloat = 0
```

Once the pan gesture assumes its starting state, one can begin to record the current progress of the animation.

```
animationProgress = transitionAnimator.fractionComplete
```

In the pan gesture's changed state, one has to add the animation progress to the calculated fraction.

```
transitionAnimator.fractionComplete = fraction + animationProgress
```

So now the pan gesture works correctly and monitors the user's finger in a natural way.

4. Introduce custom instant pan gesture

The interruption behavior works in a rather surprising manner. For the pan to get recognized, it is important for the user to touch the screen and move their finger in any given direction. One would like the action to be that of a scroll view that permits users to catch the view once they tap down. As per the moment, both the tap gesture plus pan gesture get triggered by touch up. To activate an event on the touchdown, one can create a personal custom gesture recognizer. The code is shown below:

```
class InstantPanGestureRecognizer: UIPanGestureRecognizer {
    override func touchesBegan(_ touches: Set<UITouch>, with event: UIEvent) {
        if (self.state == UIGestureRecognizerState.began) { return }
        super.touchesBegan(touches, with: event)
        self.state = UIGestureRecognizerState.began
    }
}
```

The above is a pan gesture subclass that goes to the begin state on the touchdown. It permits one to replace all the earlier gesture recognizers. The tap has become instant and ends immediately it starts. Making a choice to use this custom gesture recognizer, can enhance the behavior of the earlier tap solution so that the logic can be simplified.

5. Use pan velocity to reverse animations

There is only one problem that is yet to be solved. The popup does not follow the direction the view is "thrown". Once you tap on the closed popup, and capture its mid-animation and then swap back down, it will proceed to animate open. To solve this issue, one has to reverse the animator. This will depend on several factors some of which include the present state of the popup if the animator is currently reversed as well as the velocity of the pan gesture.

Therefore, the ended incidence of the pan gesture handler shall appear this way:

```
let yVelocity = recognizer.velocity(in: popupView).y
let shouldClose = yVelocity > 0
if yVelocity == 0 {
    transitionAnimator.continueAnimation(withTimingParameters: nil, durationFactor: 0)
    break
}
switch currentState {
case .open:
    if !shouldClose && !transitionAnimator.isReversed { transitionAnimator.isReversed = !transitionAnimator.isReversed }
    if shouldClose && transitionAnimator.isReversed { transitionAnimator.isReversed = !transitionAnimator.isReversed }
case .closed:
    if shouldClose && !transitionAnimator.isReversed { transitionAnimator.isReversed = !transitionAnimator.isReversed }
    if !shouldClose && transitionAnimator.isReversed { transitionAnimator.isReversed = !transitionAnimator.isReversed }
}
transitionAnimator.continueAnimation(withTimingParameters: nil, durationFactor: 0)
```

This logic can appear hard to understand but you can figure it out by taking into consideration all other possible cases. In the changed incident of the pan gesture handler, one is supposed to pay attention to the isReversed property of the animator.

```
let translation = recognizer.translation(in: popupView)
var fraction = -translation.y / popupOffset
if currentState == .open { fraction *= -1 }
if transitionAnimator.isReversed { fraction *= -1 }
transitionAnimator.fractionComplete = fraction + animationProgress
```

So far, the animation is reversed. If a user would like to close the popup mid-animation, it is easy for them to achieve that.

6. Corner radius animation

In the iOS 11, there is a CALayer's corner radius that is Animatable without the need for a CABasicAnimation. This implies that one can update the view's corner radius in the animation block and still it will work fine.

```
self.popupView.layer.cornerRadius = 20
```

It is also possible to define the corners around. In the following case, the top left and top right corners are the ones that need rounding.

```
view.layer.maskedCorners = [.layerMaxXMinYCorner, .layerMinXMinYCorner]
```

So far, the top two corners have been animated besides the original animation.

7. Improve its elegance

The gray popup view works better, however, some visual improvements make it look better. You can add a background image as the overlay view, a subtitle shadow, title label, and sample reviews.

8. Label animation

There is no built-in method that one can animate a label's color or the font style. The way is achieved is through a simple workaround. To make the transition smooth, one is supposed to animate the scale and translation of every label so that it can overlap in the whole length of the animation.

9. Refactoring for multiple animators

This label animation will operate correctly, however, one could improve the timing so that the transition becomes more smooth. To alter the timing curve of the label animations, you require extra animators. That is the UIViewPropertyAnimator which has one timing curve. This means that for one to use multiple curves, it is a must to integrate multiple animators.

It is important to refactor the code a little so that one can support several animators. To achieve this one, an array of animators is created as shown below:

```
private p var runningAnimators = [UIViewPropertyAnimator]()
```

Once a new animator is created, it is added to the array of running animators.

```
runningAnimators.append(transitionAnimator)
```

When the animation ends, one can remove it from the array. To enable the remaining code to work with the multiple animators, anything that is going to be used on the transitionAnimator has to be applied to the whole array.

10. Create new animators for the alpha label

With the new infrastructure, one can create two new animators to animate the new label in and another one to animate the old label out. The advantage of having multiple animators is that everything has its own timing curve.

```
let inTitleAnimator = UIViewPropertyAnimator(duration: duration, curve: .easeIn, animations: {
    switch state {
    case .open:
        self.openTitleLabel.alpha = 1
    case .closed:
        self.closedTitleLabel.alpha = 1
    }
})
inTitleAnimator.scrubsLinearly = false
```

In this example, the animator's scrubsLinearly property is set to false to make the fraction completed of the animation to be mapped to the ease-in timing curve. In general, animations which emulate the finger of the user should assume a linear timing curve. And that is the reason why this property is true by default.

The difference is small but it will permit the animation to get customized further in the near future. Ensuring that one gets this transition right is essential when the user has complete control over the animation and can also scrub it to a given point.

Chapter 9

Create a today widget in Swift Language

The most popular feature in iOS 8 is the ability to develop different types of extensions. This Chapter will take you through the process of building a custom widget for the Today section notification center. First, you will get to learn some few topics related to the extensions and learn important topics about widgets.

Definition of an extension

An extension refers to a unique binary. Don't confuse it with a complete app because it still requires a containing app as a distribution. This may be an existing app that has one or more extensions. Even though extensions aren't distributed independently, it has its own container.

The extension is activated and controlled in the host app. It might be a Safari if you are building a share extension or even a Today system app that manages notification and other widgets. Every system area that allows extension is referred to as an extension point.

To build an extension, one is supposed to develop a target to the project of the containing app. The templates that exist in the Xcode have the right frameworks for every extension point. This allows the app to interact with and stick to the right policies of the host app.

The Today extension

Extensions that have been built for today extension point are referred to as widgets. These have been developed to supply a simple and quick access to information. The widgets connect to the Notification Centre framework. Every developer is advised to design a widget using a simple and focused user interface because a lot of interaction can create a problem. You should also know that you don't have access to a keyboard.

Widgets are meant to perform well and ensure that the content remains updated. Performance is an important aspect that should be considered. A widget is supposed to be available quickly and make use of resources in the best way possible. This will prevent bringing down the whole experience. The system stops widgets that have excess memory. It is important that a widget is simple and focused towards the content it displays.

Let's now create a custom today widget. The widget that is being created will display information related to disk usage as well as a progress bar to deliver a fast visual experience for the user. There are also other important concepts of the iOS 8 extensions that shall be covered.

The Target Setup

1. **Setting up the Project**

When you want to create a widget extension to an app that is already existing, navigate and open the Xcode project and go straight to the second step. However, if you are beginning from scratch, then you have to start by building a containing app.

To create a containing app, open the Xcode and go to the File menu. In the file menu, click New > Target.

While in the iOS tab, select the "Today Extension "template then click next. Fill the Product Name and choose the correct "Embed in Application" Target.

In the Extension Target General Tab, you can decide to set the Version as well as the Build so that it matches the main iOS of the project to prevent the warning below from arising.

"CFBundleVersion Mismatch and CFBundleShortVersionString Mismatch"

Remove Storyboards

In case you don't want to use storyboards, you can choose to delete the "MainInterface. Storyboard" file. Starting from Info.plist, you can go to the NSExtension directory and delete the NSExtensionMainStoryboard key. Add a new key to the NSExtension dictionary named "NSExtensionPrincipalClass" and select the main "ViewController.swift" which matches the NCWidgetProviding protocol.

You can also add @objc(ViewController) tag to the top of the View Controller class to prevent any error such as "Terminating app due to uncaught exception 'NSInvalidArgumentException', reason: '*** setObjectForKey: object cannot be nil".

Import Pods

If you want to apply cocoa pods in the widget, you can add the new widget target into the Podfile plus a new target. The example below will show the SnapKit pod to the "TodayExtension" widget.

```
target 'TodayExtension' do
    platform :ios, '9.0'
    use_frameworks!
    pod 'SnapKit', '~> 3.2.0'
end
```

Create the View

One can still apply the auto layout to develop the today widget view. The width of this widget is constant. The today widget comes compact both in size and contains a fixed height of 110pts. However, the user can still click "Show More" on the widget so that they can expand and "show less" to minimize it. While in the show more state, the widget can contain variable height that extends to the screen size.

If you want to know when the user has altered the display mode, you can implement the function below:

```
func widgetActiveDisplayModeDidChange(_
activeDisplayMode: NCWidgetDisplayMode,
withMaximumSize maxSize: CGSize)
```

It is possible to check the active display mode and retrieve the maximum width and heights present. In case you are in the expanded state, you can make use of the. expanded rather than. compact.

Entitlements

When you want to share data between the today widget and the host application, you might need to add the "App Groups" entitlement. Go to the project and navigate to your widget's Target and choose the Capabilities Tab. Switch on the App Groups and add a new App Group using a unique name such as "group.com.domain.app". Navigate to the container application's Capabilities and activate the App Groups, choose the same app group that you had created earlier.

Now you can share the data between the two apps by using a UserDefaults suite name.

The Custom URL

In case you would like to tap on the Today Widget or even open the container/host application, then you must be ready to create a custom URL scheme. Simply follow the first step and register the custom URL scheme.

Chapter 10

UICollectionView Custom Layout

The UICollectionView exists from iOS 6. It is a popular UI element to all iOS developer. The reason why it is such an amazing resource is that it separates data and presentation layers. This depends on a different object to manage the layout. The layout is then responsible for defining the placement and visual attributes of the views.

There is a great chance that you might have applied the default flow layout that exists in the UIKit. This contains a normal grid layout plus a few customizations. However, one can organize the views in whichever way they want, this tends to make the collection view powerful and flexible.

This chapter will take you through the process of creating a layout that is similar to the Pinterest app.

The Pinterest app contains a gallery of photos. With the app, you are able to browse the photos. The gallery has been created with the help of a collection view that has a standard layout.

Create a custom collection view layout

The first thing to do when you want to develop a stunning collection view is ensuring that you have a custom layout class for the gallery. The collection view layouts include subclasses of the abstract UICollectionViewLayout class. This often defines the visual properties of each item in the collection view. The individual features represent the instances of the UICollectionViewLayoutAttributes and it has properties of every item in the collection view. That includes the item's transform and frame.

Develop a new file in the Layouts group. Click Cocoa Touch Class by navigating to the iOS\Source list. Assign it the name Pinterest layout and create a subclass of the UICollectionViewLayout. You should ensure that the language used is Swift before you can create the file.

The next thing is to develop a collection view that can use a new layout. Click the Main.storyboard and choose Collection View while in the Photo Stream View Controller Scene. This is shown in the figure below:

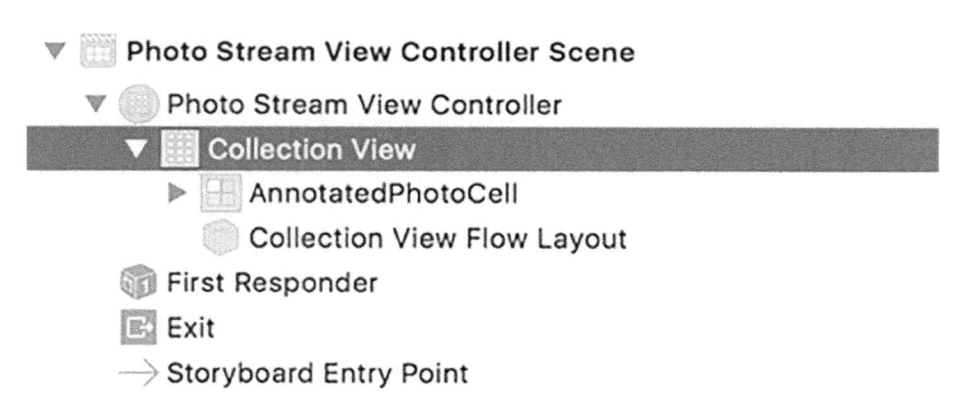

- ▼ Photo Stream View Controller Scene
  - ▼ Photo Stream View Controller
    - ▼ **Collection View**
      - ▶ AnnotatedPhotoCell
      - Collection View Flow Layout
  - First Responder
  - Exit
  - → Storyboard Entry Point

The next thing is to open the Attributes Inspector and choose Custom while in the Layout drop-down list. Here you can move on and click PinterestLayout while in the Class drop-down list.

Collection View

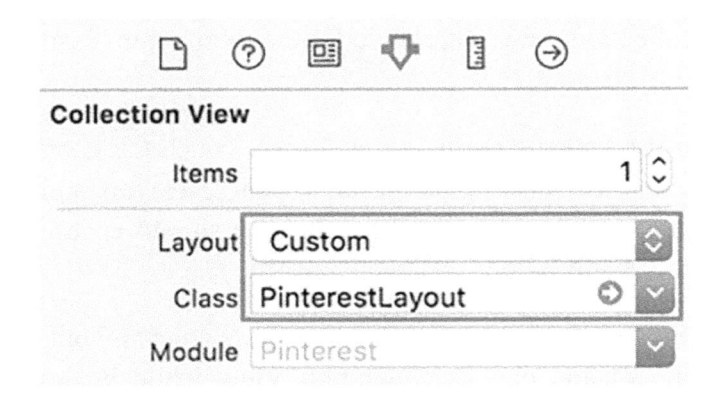

Items	1
Layout	Custom
Class	PinterestLayout
Module	Pinterest

Then you can build and run to get a look at how it will appear.

Core Layout Process

Take some time and consider the collection view layouts process that is a combination between the layout object and collection view. Anytime the collection view requires information related to the layout, it will request the layout object to deliver specific methods in a given order.

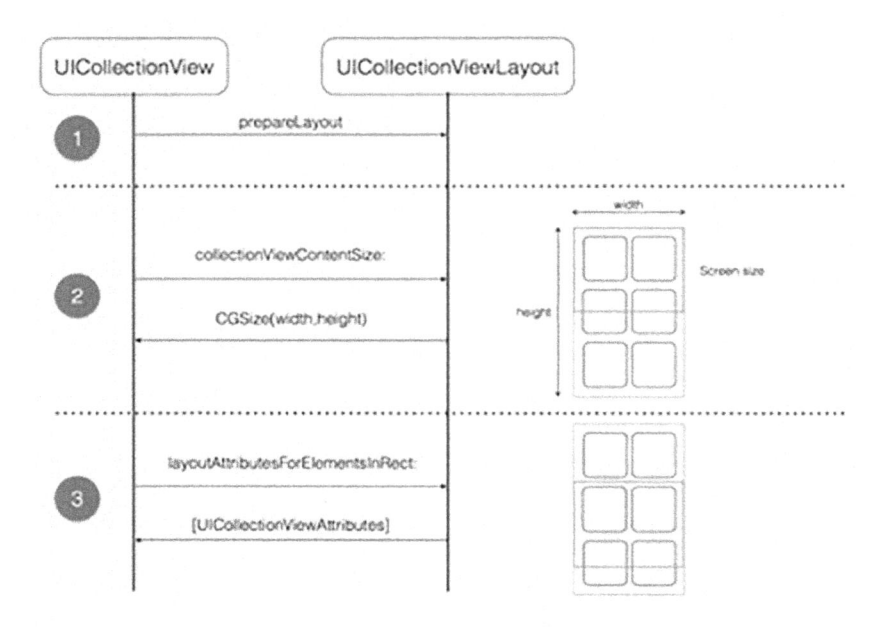

138

The layout subclass has to implement the following methods:

1. Prepare (): This method is applied when a layout operation is going to take place. It is the role of the developer to perform the calculations needed to define the collection view's size as well as the position of the items.

2. CollectionViewContentSize: This method will present the width and height of the collection view's contents. One has to override it and return the width and height of the whole collection view's content. The collection view has internal information that can be used to configure the scroll view's content size.

3. LayoutAttributesForElements(in). This method requires one to return an attribute of layout for every item in the rectangle. The attributes are returned to collection view in form of an array of UICollectionViewLayoutsAttributes.

4. LayoutAttributesForItem(at): This method offers a high demand layout information to the collection view. One is supposed to override it and go back to the layout attributes for all the items that have been requested by the indexPath.

How can you calculate the attributes?

To calculate attributes for this particular layout, one has to dynamically calculate the height of each item because nobody knows what the height of the photo can turn out to be. One has to declare a protocol that will supply information to the Pinterest layout when it wants.

To return to the code. First, you should open Pinterest layout.swift and add the protocol declaration below before the Pinterest layout class.

```
protocol PinterestLayoutDelegate: class {
  func collectionView(_
  collectionView:UICollectionView,
  heightForPhotoAtIndexPath indexPath:IndexPath) ->
  CGFloat
}
```

In this code, PinterestLayoutDelegate protocol is declared. It has a method that asks for the height of the photo. This protocol is implemented in PhotoStreamViewController.

There is just one thing that one can do before they can implement the layout methods. An individual has to declare some properties that will be important to the layout process. To achieve that, add the code below to the Pinterest layout:

```
weak var delegate: PinterestLayoutDelegate!

// 2
fileprivate var numberOfColumns = 2
fileprivate var cellPadding: CGFloat = 6

// 3
fileprivate var cache = [UICollectionViewLayoutAttributes]()

// 4
fileprivate var contentHeight: CGFloat = 0

fileprivate var contentWidth: CGFloat {
  guard let collectionView = collectionView else {
    return 0
  }
  let insets = collectionView.contentInset
  return collectionView.bounds.width - (insets.left + insets.right)
}

// 5
override var collectionViewContentSize: CGSize {
  return CGSize(width: contentWidth, height: contentHeight)
}
```

This code has certain properties defined that one will require to supply information to the layout. This is explained below step-by-step:

1. It maintains a reference to the delegate
2. There are two properties that help one configure the layout. The cell padding and a number of columns.
3. It is an array where calculated attributes are cached. Once you call prepare(), you need to calculate the attributes for every item and add it to the cache. When the time comes for the collection view to ask for the layout attributes, one is supposed to be efficient and query the cache rather than recalculate each time.
4. It declares two properties for the content size. The contentHeight is increased when photos are added, and the width of the content is calculated depending on the collection view width.
5. It overrides the CollectionViewContentSize method that returns the size of the collection view's contents. One can apply both the contentHeight and contentWidth from other steps to help calculate the size.

Now you can start to calculate the attributes of the collection view items that will comprise of the frame. Take a look at the following diagram to help you understand how to do it.

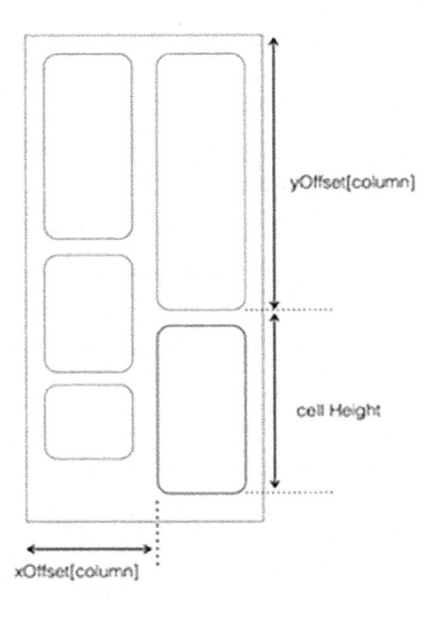

So you will need to calculate the frame of each item depending on the column offset and the position of the earlier item that is monitored by yOffset.

If you want to calculate the horizontal position, you have to begin with the X coordinate of the column item and then add a cell padding. The vertical position represents the starting point of the previous item in the column and height of the previous item. The height of the general item is the sum of content padding and image height.

This is done to prepare (). Add the method below to the Pinterest layout:

```swift
override func prepare() {
    // 1
    guard cache.isEmpty == true, let collectionView = collectionView else {
        return
    }
    // 2
    let columnWidth = contentWidth / CGFloat(numberOfColumns)
    var xOffset = [CGFloat]()
    for column in 0 ..< numberOfColumns {
        xOffset.append(CGFloat(column) * columnWidth)
    }
    var column = 0
    var yOffset = [CGFloat](repeating: 0, count: numberOfColumns)

    // 3
    for item in 0 ..< collectionView.numberOfItems(inSection: 0) {

        let indexPath = IndexPath(item: item, section: 0)

        // 4
        let photoHeight = delegate.collectionView(collectionView, heightForPhotoAtIndexPath: indexPath)
        let height = cellPadding * 2 + photoHeight
        let frame = CGRect(x: xOffset[column], y: yOffset[column], width: columnWidth, height: height)
        let insetFrame = frame.insetBy(dx: cellPadding, dy: cellPadding)

        // 5
        let attributes = UICollectionViewLayoutAttributes(forCellWith: indexPath)
        attributes.frame = insetFrame
        cache.append(attributes)
```

```swift
        // 6
        contentHeight = max(contentHeight, frame.maxY)
        yOffset[column] = yOffset[column] + height

        column = column < (numberOfColumns - 1) ? (column + 1) : 0
    }
}
```

Let's explain the above code based on the numbered comments

1. The layout attributes are calculated only when the cache is empty and the collection view exists.
2. It declares and populates the xOffset array using x-coordinate for each column depending on the width of the column. The yOffset array shall monitor the y-position for each column. Then you can initialize every value in the yOffset to 0.
3. This will rotate around all items existing in the first section since this layout has one section.
4. The frame calculations happen here. Width has been calculated previously and cell padding between cells omitted.
5. This builds an instance of the UICollectionViewLayoutAAttribute. Then it defines the frame with the help of the insetFrame and joins the attributes to the cache.

6. In this line, the contentHeight is expanded to make up for the frame of the newly calculated item. It will then expand the yOffset of the current column depending on the frame. Lastly, it expands the column so that the next item is placed inside the column.

The most important thing to remember is that while prepare () is called, there are a lot of cases in a normal implementation where one may require to calculate the attributes. So you will require to override layoutAttributesForElements(in). This is what the collection view calls after prepare() to define elements that are visible in a specific rect.

Add this code at the end of the PinterestLayout:

```
override func layoutAttributesForElements(in rect: CGRect) -> [UICollectionViewLayoutAttributes]? {
    var visibleLayoutAttributes = [UICollectionViewLayoutAttributes]()
    // Loop through the cache and look for items in the rect
    for attributes in cache {
        if attributes.frame.intersects(rect) {
            visibleLayoutAttributes.append(attributes)
        }
    }
    return visibleLayoutAttributes
}
```

Here one is supposed to iterate through the attributes in the cache and confirm whether the frames intersect with the rect. Then you can add any type of attributes with frames that intersect with the rect to layoutAttributes. Eventually, this is returned back to the collection view.

The last method that needs to be implemented is the layoutAttributesForItem (at:)

```
override func layoutAttributesForItem(at indexPath: IndexPath) -> UICollectionViewLayoutAttributes? {
    return cache[indexPath.item]
}
```

In this case, you will need to retrieve and go back to the cache layout attributes that are similar to the requested indexPath.

Before you get to see how the layout operates, you require to implement the layout delegate. PinterestLayout depends on this to create photo and annotation heights when you want to calculate the heights of an attribute frame.

Now, open the PhotoStreamViewController. Swift and add the extension below to the end of the file so that it can accept the PinterestLayoutDelegate protocol.

```swift
extension PhotoStreamViewController: PinterestLayoutDelegate {
    func collectionView(_ collectionView: UICollectionView,
                        heightForPhotoAtIndexPath indexPath:IndexPath) -> CGFloat {
        return photos[indexPath.item].image.size.height
    }
}
```

Lastly, add the code below inside viewDidLoad (), it should be below the super:

```swift
if let layout = collectionView?.collectionViewLayout as? PinterestLayout {
    layout.delegate = self
}
```

This will set the PhotoStreamViewController to be the delegate for the layout.

Finally, you can build and run the app to see how the cells get positioned and sized depending on the heights of the photos.

Chapter 11

Get Directions and Draw routes in Swift

Directions and Draw routes in Swift

This chapter will guide you on how to draw a route map on the Mapkit between two points using Swift language. You will use MKAnnotation's to draw the pins for source and destination. To get the route, one has to use MKDirection class and create a polyline on the MkMapView. Use the steps below to help you learn how you can draw a route between places on the MKMapView.

1. Create a fresh project called 'DrawRouteOnMapKit'. Navigate to the "Main.storyboard" and drag the 'Map Kit view' to the view.

2. While on the "ViewController. Swift", develop an IBOutlet of the map kit view.

3. Open 'Main.storyboard' and create a link between the mapkitview in the first step.

4. Next, open the 'ViewController. Swift', this is the time you need to develop a class for the pins. Also, MKAnnotations will act as a pole for the source and destination location.

5. Now that you have created a custom class successfully for the pin. This is the time to determine direction between two locations and draw a route on the Mapkit. Go to the ViewDidLoad, then

create coordinates for the source location and destination location.

6. Next is to use a custom MKAnnotation class and develop pins for the source and destination locations using coordinates defined in the last step.

7. If you choose to build and run the app at this point, two points will show up on the map.

8. To get the direction for routes between two points, you must develop a placemark with the help of the MKPlaceMark class that accepts coordinate. Two placemarks for the source and destination location will be created.

9. To find the directions, use the MKDirectionRequest class. The MKDirectionRequest class has features such as the destination, transportType and source. Finally, use the MKDirection class and determine the directions. You will receive directions in the callback. Here is the final code. Build and run the app so that you can see the pins without a route. Therefore, you will need to create a delegate method for the MapKit to help you render the route.

10. Define the delegate of the mapview to self and implement the delegate method.

Conclusion

You have successfully completed Swift for Intermediate Programmers. You have learned how to build adaptive user interfaces for your iPhone apps. So far, you know how to animate table views in cells. You don't have to worry when it comes to JSON and Codable in swift because you know what to do and how you can do it. All the way, you have covered different things related to creating apps in Swift.

Until now, you can combine most of the features learned in this book and develop a Swift application. Besides that, you can apply your own knowledge and understanding to write some simple iOS applications and Mac OS X applications.

Programming in Swift language is by far the most exciting thing. As you may realize, Apple had several reasons to build and launch this language for the iOS platform. One of the reasons is to help new developers approach their platform with some ease and increase both the stability and safety of their applications. Therefore, as a Swift developer, you can be sure that you will build apps that are safe and secure. Think of Swift as a scripting language that has both the elements of functional programming and object-oriented programming.

That said, it is important to know that you have just started. Keep moving forward. Don't stop here. Get other advanced Swift books and expand your knowledge of Swift programming. Remember. This book has only covered major areas in Swift app design. There are still plenty of topics that you need to master.

SWIFT

Advanced Detailed Approach To Master Swift Programming with Latest Updates

Introduction

Swift is currently an open source programming language. The purpose is to build a great programming language by offering access to technology to everyone. Therefore, after three years since it was released, Swift has already won a large community and several third-party tools.

The main benefit that Swift provides is safety, but it also focuses on improving the code so that it looks natural.

Over the last two or three years, there has been a massive dominance of Swift over Objective-C both in customer development projects and in-house projects. Since the language was made open source in 2015, there have been three key upgrades, each bringing a backward-incompatible language format changes. Although this has increased the workload of the library maintenance, each change has made it even better.

Compared to its "predecessor," the creation of Swift has been pretty faster. It is less verbose and more expressive. The syntax is great and consistent — no need for the block syntax type of cheat sheet. In the current state, developing a strong code has turned out to be less error-prone than using Objective-C. The new version of Swift Language brings some of the best additions to data with, especially with ABI (Application Binary Interface) stability as the main feature. Just like the API, the ABI is a type of interface that is well-defined and important for integrating software entities.

Other features introduced include small changes to the String class and more related to the standard APIs. In this book, we shall take you through the changes that we're introduced in both Swift version 4.2 and version 5.0. Stay tuned for more.

Chapter 1

Swift Latest Updates

A new version of the Swift programming language, which was slated to be released in early 2019 is now released. Yes! Now you can begin to enjoy programming with Swift 5.0. Swift 5.0 is a major step in the evolution of the Swift language. Thanks to the ABI stability, the Swift runtime is now part of the current and future version of Apple's platform OS: iOS, macOS, tvOS and watchOS. The Swift 5 also comes with new capabilities that are the foundation for future versions. This comprises of enforcement of exclusive access to memory during runtime, a reimplementation of String, new data types, and support for callable types.

With the release of Swift 5.0, how does this update affect Ios development? And who's behind these changes?

In this chapter, we'll introduce you to some of the proposed and accepted changes for Swift 5.0 changes. You'll also learn how the process of making changes to the Swift language occurs, and why it is important for iOS programmers.

The goal of this chapter is to walk you through a comprehensive list of the Swift 5.0 changes, but also to give you some ideas into how the Swift language is being developed. It is also a great opportunity for Swift programmers to learn more about Swift, and what is involved in the development of a programming language.

That said, why don't we start?

How is the Swift 5.0 Update implemented?

The Swift programming language first introduced in 2014. It is a stable language used in the development of apps, but the language is continuously being developed. Five years later, we're at version 5.0.

At the end of 2015, the Swift language became an open source language. In other words, anyone can read, modify, and copy the source code that makes the Swift language. Since then, the open source community has been actively improving the language, with over 600+ contributors.

Swift language was initially the "second" language for apps in the Apple ecosystem (watchOS, IOS, tvOS) next to Objective –C. Since it's open source, you can use it on different platforms, in particular, Ubuntu and Linux. This resulted in the rise of server-side Swift using Swift as a back-end language for development of web services.

It's important to understand that Swift is bigger than building iOS apps, and as you are going to see soon, this is especially true for Swift 5.0.

In other words, changes to the Swift programming language follow this process:

- Updates to the language are proposed and discussed on a GitHub repository known as Swift Evolution.

- Anyone can recommend changes to the language, but there's a protocol that has to be followed. You will discover that many changes are first discussed in the Swift Forums, and other related communities.

- The proposed changes are then publicly reviewed by the Swift core team, including Apple engineers like Ted Kremenek and Chris Lattner. A list comprising of current and past proposals can be accessed on the Swift Evolution.

- Proposals usually involve technical designs or written source code. Later, when a proposal is accepted, the source code for the change is integrated into the Swift source code.

- Of course, not all proposals are accepted, some are rejected. If you want to look at a rejected proposal, you can go to SE-0217, that is about bang operator. It is a great proposal that is easy to understand and has triggered good discussions and insights within the Swift developer community. It's a great example to show that Swift Evolution is beyond just coming up with a great programming language.

An excellent primer to understand the Swift Evolution is to take time and go through the Commonly Rejected Changes document. This document describes the changes to the Swift languages that have been constantly suggested but then rejected by the core Swift team, and the reason why it was rejected. They're easy to understand, even for new developers, so it's a good thing to work your way through them if you're getting started to the Swift language and the operations of Swift Evolution.

How can you scan through the Swift Evolution repository? Searching through the proposal directory is easy. Scroll down to check the most recent proposals. Some of the commit messages include Swift 5, so it will be easy to filter them out. You can as well clone the repository on your local computer and text-search the proposals using tags such as "Status: Implemented(Swift5)".

So far you know something about the development of Swift language, now it's time to dive into Swift 5.0.

The Purpose of Swift 5.0: ABI Stability

Before you get to understand more about Swift 5.0 ABI Stability, let's briefly discuss some of the pros of Swift language.

First, Swift is a safe, fast and fun language to use to code. It has a full stack capability and huge community support. The language is estimated to be 2.6 times faster than Objective-C. However, some studies show that the difference in speed is negligible. It is easy to maintain code written in the Swift language, and there are no separate implementation files and interface. Its syntax is shorter, and the language supports dynamic frameworks.

The language has been growing significantly, with many developers now learning more about Swift. According to StackOverflow, Swift is the 6th most loved language. For a language introduced in 2014, its adoption rate is remarkable.

Those are some of the pros of the Swift Language; you will better understand them if you are a developer. Now let us see some of the drawbacks from a developer's perspective. Swift is still growing, and not yet attained complete development. You can look at it as a moving target with the main changes getting introduced after every new release. One of the major problems highlighted by Swift programmers is the absence of backward compatibility with previous language versions and the version-lock. This means that there can only be one version of Swift in the whole project and it's outside dependencies.

Therefore, developers have no otherwise but to fully rewrite their projects when they want to shift to the latest Swift version and update their external dependencies. For developers who create frameworks, they need to update the framework for each new Swift version, and they cannot share it as a binary precompiled framework.

The ABI Stability Manifesto

The ABI Stability Manifesto mainly addresses the following key points:

1. Source Compatibility: This means that new compilers can compile code written in an older version of Swift. This excludes the version-lock that is present in the current Swift version.

2. Binary framework and runtime compatibility. This will support the distribution of frameworks in a binary form that operates across numerous Swift versions. The binary framework compatibility will be realized by module format stability, which improves the module file. This is a compiler's representation of the public interfaces of a framework and ABI stability supports binary compatibility between applications and libraries designed with various Swift versions.

What is ABI?

At runtime, the Swift program libraries work hand in hand with other libraries and components. Application Binary Interface is the definition to which binary entities compiled independently must conform to be joined and executed. These binary entities have to conform on various low-level details such as how to call functions, representation of data in memory, and where their metadata is and the way to access it.

ABI stability refers to the locking down of the ABI to the point where any future compiler versions can generate binaries that conform to the stable ABI. If the ABI is stable, it will persist for the entire lifetime of the platform.

The ABI stability only changes the invariants of externally visible public interfaces and symbols. For instance, the future compilers can change the calling conventions for internal function calls as long as the public interfaces are preserved.

Requirements of ABI Stability

1. Types, for instance, structs and classes, must feature an in-memory layout definition for instances that have similar layout conventions.

2. Swift programs largely use the type metadata. The following metadata has to contain a defined memory layout or even have a set of defined APIs for querying the type metadata.

3. Each exported symbol in a library requires a unique name which binary entities can conform. Swift offers function overloading and contextual namespaces. This means that any name in source code may not be globally unique. A unique name is generated through a method called name mangling.

4. Swift ships with runtime library, which controls things such as dynamic casting, reflection, reference counting, etc. Compiled Swift programs trigger external calls out to the following runtime. Therefore, Swift runtime API is Swift ABI.

5. Functions have to fulfill calling conventions, which requires things like the layout of the call stack, and ownership conventions.

6. Swift ships with a standard library that define common types, operations, and structures. For a shipped standard library to operate with applications written in various versions of Swift, it has to reveal a stable API.

As an IOS programmer, you rely on the API of a library to write a code for your apps. The UIKit framework, for instance, has an API to interface with buttons, view controllers, and labels.

You need this API as a developer, the same way you need the steering wheel to drive a car. There are private APIs like the odometer of your car. In general, the steering wheel connects to the internal wheels of your car. When you steer the car using the steering wheel "API," the car turns.

How the steering wheel links up with the car's wheels is the Application Binary Interface (ABI). Inside, the steering wheel joins a shaft between the wheels of the car, which turns the wheels. You cannot direct or regulate the working of the following system. The only thing that you can do is to steer.

Therefore, when a user downloads and installs your app, they will not download all the code that your app requires to execute correctly. A big percentage of that code is already set up in their iPhone, as part of the operating system, and it's libraries and frameworks. This means that your app will use the binary code that is available, through the ABI.

Now suppose your app has a different version of a specific framework? A different version implies different APIs and ABIs. Luckily, most versions of IOS are both backward and forward compatible, at least for several IOS versions. Apps that have been compiled with the IOS 11 SDK operate on IOS 10, and some exceptions apply.

Let's return to Swift now.

Previously, the challenge posted by Swift is that it has an unstable Application Binary Interface. The language isn't stable to come as part of IOS, like other libraries and frameworks.

ABI stability, in this case, means that future compilers of Swift language will require to generate binaries that can work on stable ABI that belongs to IOS. The Swift core team isn't convinced yet that the ABI is stable to be transferred as part of IOS; however, with the release of Swift 5.0, everything has now changed.

Until this point, the solution has always been to transfer IOS apps that have Swift using the Swift dynamic binary itself. Rather than connect to the OS, each app connects to its specific version of Swift.

The main advantage now is that IOS developers can build apps using Swift, while Swift is actively being developed, without running the risk of ABI incompatibility. Changes to Swift can be transferred without the need to update the IOS.

While it's advantageous, there are also drawbacks to it:

- If the ABI is stable, vendors of the operating system can securely include the Swift binary interface with releases of their operating system. This usually affects the adoption of Swift beyond the Apple ecosystem.

- Each Swift app comes with a version of the Swift dynamic libraries. This consumes storage space and bandwidth. In other words, it is a waste of resources.

- Developers can now be able to share pre-compiled frameworks. Thus, you don't need to compile a library before you use it, which impacts Xcode compile times, but also prepares a way for Swift-based commercial libraries and binary packages for Linux.

- A stable ABI implies that the language cannot change in many ways, and less frequent, because the Swift library is shipped using IOS. If you still recall the Swift 2 to 3 migration, this is a great thing.

In brief, ABI stability is a significant step for Swift "growing up" and becoming more mainstream beyond IOS. It's also a necessity for companies and products shifting to Swift-only apps and libraries.

Now, let's look at some actual Swift 5.0 changes.

Integer Multiples using "isMultiple(of:)"

One of the most common uses in practical programming is testing whether a number is divisible by another number. Many of these tests require a person to determine whether a number is even or odd.

The default strategy is to apply the remainder operator %. The code below determines whether the remainder of 5 divided by two is equivalent to 0. The answer is not because the remainder is 1. Therefore, 5 is an odd number.

```
let result = 5 % 2 == 0
print(result)
// Output: false
```

This proposed change implements a new function isMultiple(of:) for integers that determines whether a given number is a multiple of another number.

Below is how you can use it:

```
let number = 42

if number.isMultiple(of: 2) {
    print("\(number) is even!")
}
```

The reasons to include it in the Swift standard library is:

- It improves the readability of the code because the sentences appear like common English: "if the number is multiple of 2"

- Functions can be discovered by application of code completion in Xcode so that it can assist developers who don't know the % operator, or can't see it.

- It's not common to commit mistakes using the % operator, and its execution is different across languages that a developer can use.

It's relevant to say that the above addition to the Swift language reveals why changes to the languages are done. It's not only about "better," but "better for whom?" Who will benefit when the community adds this function to the language?

This new isMultiple (of:) function doesn't perform better than %. But what does it mean to be "better?" In this case, it is safe, easy to discover, convenience for developers and improves readability.

The result type

It is a pretty cool feature because it will add an entirely new type to the Swift: Result.

You are already familiar with errors in Swift using do-try-catch. You also know that most functions still pass Error or NSError values from async APIs, for instance.

The result type includes two states of a passed result: failure or success. Since this type is widely applied, it has been added to the standard library.

The solution includes:

```
public enum Result<Success, Failure: Error> {
    case success(Success), failure(Failure)
}
```

This code describes an enumeration using two cases: Success and .failure. These two cases contain related types of Success and Failure. Each type in the following case is generic. Therefore Success can include any value, but the value that you send to Failure has to conform to the Error protocol.

In other words, the Result type can now be implemented as an argument passed in a completion handler for an async function call. For instance:

```
dataTask(with: url) { (result: Result<Data, Error>) in
    switch result {
    case let .success(data):
        handleResponse(data: data)
    case let .error(error):
        handleError(error)
    }
}
```

The Result type comprises of possible return values and errors in a single object. Additionally, it applies the power of enumerations to assist a person to write expressive code. For instance, a switch block that gracefully handles return values and errors.

This update to Swift is perhaps more involved than adding a new convenient function, so it is essential to study it further. You can even refer to it as philosophical. The designers of Swift language discuss how the language is implemented, instead of creating the syntax of Swift.

Dealing with Future Enum Cases

The update to this change involves:

- When you "switch" to an "enum," you'll have to do it comprehensively. This means you will have to add a switch case for all the case in the enumeration.

- You might have to add a case to an enum in future, which is a code-breaking update for any switch that includes an enum.

Shifting enums has to be done exhaustively. As a result, when you add a new case to an enum that's switched over, the code that you wrote earlier will break because the switch has stopped being exhaustive. It has to include the new enum case.

This is a bit cumbersome for code from libraries, frameworks, and SDKs because each time you're adding a new case to an enum you are going to break someone els' code. Also, a code-breaking change will highly affect binary compatibility.

Consider the following enum, for instance:

```swift
enum Fruit {
    case apple
    case orange
    case banana
}
```

We write a few lines of code to deal with this enumeration, to buy different fruits:

```swift
let fruit = ...

switch fruit {
case .apple:
    print("Purchasing apple for $0.50")
case .orange:
    print("Purchasing orange for $0.39")
case default:
    print("We don't sell that kind of fruit here.")
}
```

The **switch** statement in this block is exhaustive, because we have included the default. But, if you decided to include all three. Orange, .apple and .banana cases, and you or a different developer adds a new case to Fruit; the code would crash.

The solution is two-fold.

- Enumerations in the Swift standard library, and borrowed from the different place can either be frozen or non-frozen. A frozen enumeration is difficult to change in the future. On the other hand, a non-frozen enum can change in the future; this means you'll have to handle it.

- When you switch over a non-frozen enum to one that can change later, you need to include a "catch-all" default case that is similar to any values that the switch doesn't match. If you don't apply default when you are supposed to, you'll see a warning.

This generates another problem: how can you tell whether your default will match the value that you explicitly don't want to match, or that is a new enum value that has been added later? The Swift compiler isn't aware of this either, so it can't send you a warning to notify you of non-matched cases in a switch block.

Let's assume that a new fruit case is created and added to Fruit, such as. pineapple. How can you tell that you can sell the piece of fruit but won't, or that are newly added by the framework and that we can consider selling it? Swift has no method to differentiate between these cases, and it can't alert us about it.

In the Swift 5.0, a new @unknown keyword can be included in the default switch case. This doesn't alter the behaviour of default, so this case will still match any cases that can't be handled in the remaining switch block.

```
switch fruit {
case .apple:
    ...
case @unknown default:
    print("We don't sell that kind of fruit here.")
}
```

The @unknown keyword will activate a warning in the Xcode if you're handling with a possible non-exhaustive Switch statement, as a result of a changed enumeration. You can consider the following new case, thanks to the alert that wasn't possible with just *default*.

And the best thing is that because *default* works, your code can't break if new cases are added to the enum-but you receive a warning.

Flatten Nested Options with "try?"

Nested options are..unique. For instance:

```
let number:Int?? = 5
print(number)
// Output: 5
```

In the above *number* constant, it has been doubly wrapped using optional, and its type is int?? or Optional<Optional<int>>. Though it's fine to have the nested optionals, it can also be confusing.

Swift has different ways to eliminate the situation of ending up with nested optionals, for instance in *casting with as* and in *optional chaining*. But, when you use to *try? To* change errors to optionals, there's a chance to end up with nested optionals.

Below is an example:

```
let car:Car? = ...
let engine   = try? car?.getEngine()
```

In this example, a car is optional of type Car?. On the second line, we're making use of optional chaining because the car is optional. The return value of the above expression car?.getEngine() is optional too, as a result of the optional chaining. It has a type of Engine?

When you combine it using try? whose return value is also optional, you receive a double or nested optional. Therefore, the type of engine is Engine??. And this will trigger problems because to receive the value(or not) you will need to unwrap twice.

Since *as?* Already flattens optionals, one way to exit the nested optionals is to use this bit of code:

```
if let engine = (try? car?.getEngine()) as? Engine {
    // OMG!
}
```

The code optional casts Engine?? to Engine, which will then flatten the optionals because of the way as? operates. The cast itself is useless because we are working with Engine type anyway.

So you may ask –why not just make a try? Operate the same way as as? This is exactly what the new changes do. It flattens nested optionals from try?, providing it with the same behaviour as as? And optional chaining.

New "compactMapValues()" Function for Dictionaries

The Swift standard library contains two important functions for arrays and dictionaries:

- The map(_:) function involves a function to array items and will return the resulting array, while the compactMap(_:) function will also ignore nil array items.

- The mapValues(_:) function operates the same for dictionaries. It includes a function to dictionary values, and returns the dictionary-but it doesn't contain a nil counterpart.

The new updates change this and creates the compactMapValues(_:) function to dictionaries. This function will combine the compactMap(_:) function of arrays using the mapValues(_:) function of dictionaries, correctly mapping –and –filtering dictionary values.

Take a case where you analyzed your family members for their ages, in integer numbers, but your stupid uncle Bob did manage to spell out his age instead. Therefore, you run the following code:

```
let ages = [
    "Mary": "42",
    "Bob": "twenty-five har har har!!",
    "Alice": "39",
    "John": "22"
]

let filteredAges = ages.compactMapValues({ Int($0) })
print(filteredAges)
// Output: ["Mary": 42, "Alice": 39, "John": 22]
```

The compactMapValues(_:) function is useful in cases where you need to remove nil values from dictionary, or when you use a failable initializer to change dictionary values.

In this chapter, you have learned why and how Swift changes, and we have discussed a few examples of the Swift 5.0 updates. Fortunately, it's good news that Swift doesn't change that much, but some of the changes are code-breaking.

The primary purpose of Swift 5.0 is to attain ABI stability, and so far you know what that means. It's now easy to package Swift with an operating system, and it's a huge milestone for the maturity of the Swift language.

Chapter 2

Variable Types and Constants

Integers

These are whole numbers that have a fractional part, such 12 and -14. Integers can be signed or unsigned.

Swift has both signed and unsigned integers. The integers have a specific naming rule same as the language C. Like many other versions in Swift; the above integers have a capitalized name.

Integer bounds

It is possible to use the lowest and highest values of each integer type by applying the min and max features.

```
let minValue = UInt8.min   // minValue is equal to 0, and is of type UInt8
let maxValue = UInt8.max   // maxValue is equal to 255, and is of type UInt8
```

The values of the following features are the right-sized number type, and thus the expressions can be applied together with other types of values.

Int

In most cases, it's not necessary to select a particular size of integer to include in the code. Swift has extra integer type, Int, which contains the same size as the current platform's native word length.

- For the 32-bit platform, the Int has a similar size as the Int32.

- For the 64-bit platform, the Int has the same size as the Int64.

It is important to always apply the Int for integer values in your source code unless you want to use a specific integer.

Variables and Constants in Swift

In swift language, constants and variables play a significant role in information storage.

Variables refer to "things" in the code such as numbers, buttons, images, and texts. Every part of the information that the app is stored in the constant variable.

Let's begin with a simple example:

Var age: int = 23

Print (age)

What's going on this code?

- On the first line, a variable called age is declared. This variable is of type Int, and then you allocate the value 42 to it.

- Next, the value of the variable is printed using the print () function.

Therefore, the value 42 is printed out. Try it!

In this example, the variable age is declared and initialized. Before you can start to use a variable, you need to declare it first, and then initialize it.

Declaring a variable in Swift is like saying, "Swift, pay attention. I'm announcing a new variable!"

While initialization is like saying, "Swift, that variable contains an initial value of 42."

The syntax used to declare and initialize a variable as stated in the previous examples is as follows:

1. Var is a keyword that describes a new variable declaration.
2. Age refers to the variable name.
3. : separates the variable type and name.
4. Int describes the type of the variable.
5. = is used to allocate a value to the variable.
6. 23 is the value of the variable.

Yu

```
         variable name
         ┌──────────┐
     var address:String = "1 Infinite Loop, Cupertino, CA 95014"
     └─┘  └──────┘ └────┘                └──────────────────────┘
   keyword  variable type                         value
```

You can still alter the value of the variable by doing this way:

Var age : Int = 23

Age = 999

Print (age)

This is what goes on in the above code:

- First, you need to declare the variable age and allocate it a value 42
- Next, change the value to 999, by applying the assignment operator.
- Finally, print the value of age using print ().

Does that really make sense?

In Swift, you can build variables using the *var* and constants using *let*. The difference between a constant and variable is that the variable can be changed once it's defined, and a constant remains the same.

A constant is declared using the let keyword as shown below:

>Let name: String ="Bob"

>Print (name)

Can you notice how the syntax is same with the previous, the slight difference comes with the keyword let. And remember that you a constant cannot be changed after it has been initialized.

If you attempt to change a constant, you will get an error.

Swift variables and constant type

Constants and variable exist of different types. Consider the following analogy of shipping containers. The shipping containers exist of different shapes and sizes. It is impossible for a house to fit in a boat-sized container.

In the Swift language, the same thing happens. The different variable types can store separate information. You can't assign a value of a specific type to a separate variable type. Additionally, once a type is determined, it cannot be reversed.

For instance:

Let name: String =" Bob"

In the above example, the name is a constant. It accepts a string type. When you allocate a value 'BOB,' which is literal.

 This is the literal value of the text "Bob." It's referred to as a "string," because it contains text.

You cannot do this way:

Let name: String = 101

The value 101 cannot be a string, but a number. You cannot allocate it to *name,* because the variable is of type String.

Swift is a "strongly-typed" programming language, what this means is that each variable in Swift requires to have a type, and the type cannot be altered once it's declared. Also, it's also type-safe; in other words, the programming language will assist you in avoiding mistakes.

You can deal with many basic types of variables in Swift, for example:

- Int for integer numbers. This refers to whole numbers that don't have fractions such as 23
- *Double* for decimal numbers. For example, numbers containing fractions such as 3.1415
- *Bool* for the Boolean logic values false and true.
- String refers to a text. For example, strings of characters such as "Alice"

In the IOS development, the Cocoa Touch SDK, can also work with a lot of types:

- UIVIEWController for view controllers.
- UISwitch for an on-off switch.
- UIButton for buttons
- CLLOcationManager for accepting GPS coordinates.

Swift has many different types, for instance, classes, structs, protocols, enums, Optionals and generics. Each of these contains its own properties, syntax and attributes, and you can apply it to the structure of the code in different ways.

Inferring types using Type Inference

Below is an example of explicit type annotation:

Var score: Int = 0

But you can also write this as follows:

Var score = 0

The reason is of type Int; Swift has determined that score contains the type Int too.

A common mistake that newbies make is to think that score should have no type.

For the type inference, it's very important because it will cause you to become productive and will make the code easy to read. There is no need to define many types explicitly, which likes to save time.

In addition, a program which can compile the code into ones and zeroes can alter the types of the variables without changing it explicitly.

Another advantage is that the program which can compile your code into ones and zeroes can change the types of your variables without the need to change them explicitly.

Chapter 3

Value Types vs Reference Types

In the Swift programming language, there is value types and other reference types. How are they different? And what changes do the following types cause to practical IOS development?

It is easy to confuse between value and reference types in Swift with "passing by value or reference," but remember that "passing" only change the arguments passed to functions. It is completely different from valuing vs reference types, though there are some elements of similarities.

The Value Types in Swift

Here's a quick refresher of the type. You are already aware that each variable, constant, and property in Swift has a type. An integer number contains an int, text string, and so forth. You can allocate a value of a given type to a constant, for instance:

    Let playerage: Int = 42

In the above case, the value 42 is of type int is allocated to a constant called playerage. The constant has been annotated using Int type-an integer. The int type is of the struct.

We can differentiate between various types, for instance, structs, enums, closures, optionals, function types, and classes. In programming, you we save items, and those items have various names, and types-thus it is easy to set apart.

It's easy to look at both "Int" and "struct" as type, but remember that *Int* refers to the name of the type, and struct is the type.

In this section, we are looking at a specific aspect of types: determining whether a type is a reference type or value type. This changes the code that you write, so it's important to understand the difference.

The easiest explanation involves *value types* which retain a unique copy of their data, while the reference types have a copy of the data. Let's look at what that really means.

Value Types in Swift

We shall start with *value types*. Below is an example that illustrates how a value type operates

```
var a = 99
var b = a
b += 1

print(a) // 99
print(b) // 100
```

This code operates exactly the way you'd expect. This is what happens:

- The first value 99 is allocated to the constant a. The type of the following constant is Int-an integer number and a value type.

- Next, a is allocated to a new constant b. This value is copied, and both a and b now retain a unique copy of the value 99.

- Then, 1 is added to b, in this case the constant b contains a value of 100. But the constant a still has 99.

- Lastly, both values are displayed.

The most important to note in this case is that the value of the "a" constant is copied to a constant b, when allocating a to b. This will precisely create a second copy of the value 99.

The insertion is evident by the fact that the value of a cannot change when 1 is added to b on line 3. We can now see that both a and b are different values. By allocating a to b correctly, you create a copy of the data. This is the trademark of a value type.

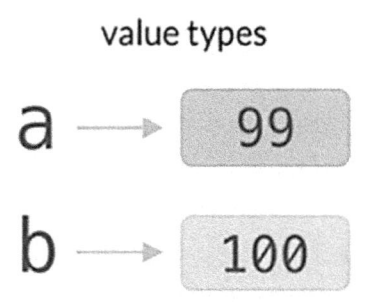

value types

a → 99

b → 100

In Swift languages, the following types contain value types:

- Structs, such as String, Int, Double, and Bool
- Arrays, sets and dictionaries.
- Enumerations and tuples.

It's safe to assume that any "primitive" type is a value type like integers and variables. Also, constructs like structs, tuples and enumerations are all value types.

The Swift programming language has support to the value types over the reference types, for some reasons. It's simple to reason about code when the value types are the default. Another thread or process can't alter a value type as you're working with it, and this will make your code less error-prone.

A great developer will highlight here that Swift doesn't blindly "copy" a value types any time you allocate it. And that's correct. Swift has different optimizations, including only copying a value it does changes. But you can end up with two identical, irrelevant copies of data. The idea of value types vs. reference types is still correct because it is not affected by optimizations in Swift.

Reference Types in Swift

The value types are copied and retain a unique copy of the data. If you change one, the other one doesn't change. Why?

The reason is that reference types operate differently. A reference type maintains a reference to a shared instance when it is allocated to a new variable or property. And this may result in all different kinds of problems.

Check out the following code:

```swift
class Car {
    var speed = 0
}

let racecar = Car()
racecar.speed = 250

let bus = racecar
bus.speed = 40

print(racecar.speed) // 40
print(bus.speed) // 40
```

Here's what is happening in the above code.

- At the top, a class called Car with a property named speed of type Int is defined. At the start, it's set to 0.

- Next, we are building an instance of Car and allocate it to a constant *racecar*.

- Next, the *speed* property is set to 250.

- Then, we assign a new constant called *the bus*. And we set the *speed* property of the *bus* to 40.

- Lastly, the *speed* property of both *racecar* and bus are printed out.

Now, evaluate whether you expected the *racecar.speed* to be 250 or 40? If you followed the previous example, it is logical to expect that when the racecar is allocated to the bus, the unique copy of the Car, for example, would be established. However, that doesn't happen here.

The *Car* type describes a *reference type* because it's a class. However, value types, reference types, aren't copied when they are allocated to a new variable, property or constant. But the reference to the instance is copied. This reference refers to the same instance, which implies that both constants refer to the same instance. You may even say that both constants have the same instance.

Swift has the following types of reference types.

- Classes
- Closures
- Functions

You should be able to see this in the above example. The Car type is a Class. When you assign r*acecar* to the *bus,* the *Car* instance is not copied. But the reference to this *Car instance is copied to the* bus. Both the racecar and bus currently refer to the same instance. This means if you change one the other one will also change.

What is a reference?

You may easily consider a "reference" as an address. A variable like *racecar,* refers to memory address that stores data for the *car* instance, The same way your home address "points to" your house.

The Value types vs reference types

- Value type: Every instance retains a unique data copy. A copy of an instance is established when it is allocated to a variable, or property.

- Reference type: Every instance has the same copy of the data. A reference to a particular instance is established when it's allocated to a variable or property.

It is simple to remember the difference by just thinking of the word "reference". For the value type, the value is copied, and for a reference type, the reference is copied.

How can you notice if a type belongs to a value or a reference type? It is easy because in Swift language, everything is a value type, not unless it's a class, closure or function.

Now, suppose a reference type has value types and vice versa?

Typically, it is ok for a reference type to have value types such as .name string. Things get complex when a value type has a reference type-for instance, one or more *Invoice* objects that point to the same *Person* object. In other words, it is easy to avoid this. If you have to, then create your own deep copy method for the reference type, or look for a great style to compare equality between two reference object types.

Mutability using "let" And "var"

If you closely check at the previous example, you'll see an odd thing. Can you see that *racecar* has been defined with *let?* That means it's a constant. Constant can't change; they are considered to be immutable by design. But how can we change it?

Var and *let* function differently for reference and value types. Here are some key points to note:

- For the reference types, it has to remain constant. When it's constant, you can change the instance, the same way properties happen, but you cannot change the reference.

- For the value types, the value itself has to stay constant. In other words, it's difficult to alter the value, or any of its properties. The value is immutable.

You can also learn from this that it's easy to control the mutability when you apply *let* and value types. Once a constant has been declared, and it's a value type, then you can be 100% sure that the data cannot change.

It is possible to change the properties of a reference type, even when it has been declared using *let*. This makes it difficult to reason about your code because of the immutability of a reference type depending on the implementation.

Practical IOS Development

Before we understand the way value types vs reference types affects the practical IOS development, it's important to look at scenarios that they matter.

- When you apply APIS, you must follow the practices of that API, including which types are value types and which one are reference types.

- When you code your own types, you must decide whether a type has to be a value type or a reference type.

Using APIs

In the first case, you will find it fairly easy to work with the value types vs. reference types. You may only have to follow along with the API. For instance, in Swift, the simplest types are the value types. When you work with the Realm, you'll see the persisted objects as the value types.

You might be surprised exactly why you're allocating a single variable to another. For the var b = an in the practical IOS development. It happens more often than you may think — every time you allocate a constant or variable to a different object's property, for instance.

A special case happens when you work with Objective-C. As you know, most types in Objective-C are bridged to Swift. For instance, the class NSString has been bridged to the struct String in Swift. The following bridging is implicit; this means that though Objective-C has a reference type only, the bridged type is considered a value type.

Creating your own APIs and types

Suppose you are developing your own classes, enums structs and tuples? At what time should you seek for a value type, such as struct, and when for a reference type such as class?

You could decide between value types vs reference types depending on:

1. How you can compare when two objects are identical or equal.

2. Whether the type contains a shared or independent state.

Determine the equality or identicality

Let's say that you are developing a DollarBill type. Should the following type be a value type like struct or a reference type like a class?

To choose, let's first determine how we're going to know that two dollar bills are similar. This can be done in two ways:

- Two dollar bills are same if they have equal monetary value such as $20. In the code, this is expressed isEqual = a. value == b. value, using the equality operator.

- Two dollar bills are equal if they point to the same physical, unique dollar bill. In the code, this is expressed as isEqual = a = == b, using the identity operator.

It is not sensible to copy dollar bills, that is why it is a great idea to select a reference type in the following case, such as class. This way, you can be 100% sure that any reference to a dollar bill points to the actual bill. When the dollar bill passes around in the code, you can be sure that no extra copies have been created. They are reference types.

Independent state

Let's consider a different example. Assume that you are developing an accounting system that has *Invoice* and *Company* types. Each invoice has a related company, to which the invoice is sent. Should the *company* and *invoice* be reference types?

Any Object in Swift

The Swift programming language has two nonspecific types referred to as Any and AnyObject. These are considered nonspecific because they can assume anything.

Here's a quick comparison. Assume that a constantly called age contains a value of 42 of type int. This type int is specific. In this case, it's clear that age is an integer number.

Now you require to look for a nonspecific type that includes Any. The code below will define *values* of array type *[any]*:

Let values: [Any] = ["Apple", 99,"zaphod",-1]

At first, it seems not to make sense but how can the *values* array include many different types, for example, Int and String? The reason is that the array type is nonspecific. In other words, it is an array-of any.

Here's another example where the individual items located in the values will apply their own specific types.

```
let values:[Any] = ["Apple", 99, "Zaphod", -1]

for value in values
{
    switch value {
    case is String:
        print("\(value) is a string!")
    case is Int:
        print("\(value) is an integer!")
    default:
        print("I don't know this value!")
    }
}
```

In this code, the for loop is implemented to help in the iteration over the items inside the *values* array. For each item we are implementing a switch block. This block will match the type value inside the three cases by implementing type checking is keyword. In particular, it will determine the type of every item within the array, and write some text based on the following type.

Well, but why are they not types Any? The type of the values array is [any]. Thus the items have to be of *any* type. Yes. And here's how:

- The array type *values* are [any]. In other words, it's nonspecific.

- The types of individual array items are specific. They include Int and String.

So, why should you apply Any using this method? Let's see:

Why implement any and any object?

The previous example causes a person to find out why would anyone have to implement *Any?*

First, understand that Swift has different characters that make it flexible in dealing with types. For instance:

- Protocols: will assist you to flexibly define the constraints for specific types, no matter the type you adopt.

- Optionals: This will assist you to handle "empty" values correctly.

- Generics: This will help you to build variables, placeholders, functions, etc., which can handle flexible types.

Realize that programming is more than generating input, processing the input, and producing output. You will be creating a code which downloads tweets from the API and changes the data, including displaying it to the user in the UI.

Therefore, it's important for Swift language to create tools and features which will make it easy for one to handle data. Generics, Optionals, type casting and protocols, are some of those tools that can effectively assist a person process data. And this often makes the code to appear clear, expressive, and easy to maintain.

AnyObject and *Any* are especially important for the value that contain nonspecific, mixed types. Take for example, this dictionary:

```
let tweet:[String: Any] = [
    "text": "Lorem ipsum dolor amet hoodie bicycle rights, 8-bit mixtape",
    "likes": 42,
    "retweets": ["@reinder42", "@aplusk", "@beeblebrox"]
]
```

Notice how the following dictionary will mix values of different types. The first value includes a string, and the second is an integer, and the last is an array of strings.

Suppose you need to find specific values in a tweet dictionary? This is how you can do it:

```
if let likes = tweet["likes"] {
    print("This tweet has \(likes) likes!")
}
```

In this code, the constant likes feature the type Int. This code implements the optional blinding to receive the value based on its key. If required, you can still make the typecast explicit. For example:

```
if let likes = tweet["like"] as? Int { ...
```

With any, you can combine the different tweet values using a single dictionary. No need to have a custom type or class for the tweet, or even apply multiple dictionaries and values. And this is super important.

The difference between *Any* and *AnyObject.*

So far you have looked at Any. But what is the difference between *Any* and *AnyObject*?

In the official Swift documentation:

- You will learn that Any can refer to any instance of any type at all, this includes the function types.

- *Anyobject describes* an instance of any class type

That looks simple, right? You apply *Any* for anything and *AnyObject* for classes. However, there's more.

It is important to note the difference between value types and reference types. In other words, a value type is copied when you pass it in code, while the reference type isn't. The classes are reference types, and by passing it around in the code, you will be creating a reference to the initial object.

This has a clear impact:

- If you change a passed value type, the original value will remain the same.
- When you change a passed reference type, the original value changes.

Next, you need to know the function of the Objective-C. This is the predecessor of Swift in Any vs AnyObject. In the Objective-C, you will see the polymorphic of the untyped id pointer to point to any type of object. Just like Any and the AnyObject in Swift language.

In the Objective-C, every object is a reference type. In other words, they can be accessed using pointers, and Objective-C doesn't hold the concept of a value type. This is a critical point.

One of the best features about Swift is the interoperability it has with the Objective-C. You can apply Objective-C code within the Swift projects and vice-versa. Additionally, you can include SDKs designed in Objective-C in the Swift projects.

The interoperability depends on joining Swift types and Objective-C types, among many other things. The Objective-C type *NSString* is linked to the Swift type string. Therefore, you can operate with strings between the two languages.

In the previous Swift versions, there was a problem when it came to importing the Objective-C.

Keep in mind that AnyObject can only operate with classes. This means that *AnyObject* belongs to the reference type. Objective-C doesn't contain value types, and the id includes a reference type because it uses pointers. This has a huge impact: you can't gain from Swift's value types when it interoperates with the Objective-C'S id.

In short, when you import Objective-C's id into Swift as AnyObject, it implies that you cannot gain from the value types in the Swift. And this the point where *Any* comes in.

As seen in other examples, the array of integers and strings has to include Any because they're value types. You can apply Any with classes, but it's better to use AnyObject.

But don't use Any when you don't want to create a value's type. It is vital to apply Any and AnyObject when you explicitly require the behaviour and the function it does. If not, you will be creating a needless ambiguity in your code.

Chapter 4

Swift Functions and For Loop

Functions can accept input and display output. They are especially important for building reusable tasks and actions in the code.

By understanding the way functions operate, it will help you understand the development of IOS apps.

How to define and Call functions

Functions can be defined as self-contained parts of a code that carry out a particular task.

Functions are like small sections of a code that you implement by calling the function's name. A function accepts input parameters and generates an output value.

Here's an analogy to consider. If you are playing a game of chess and you want to move the rook piece this way:

MoveForward(piece: rook, steps: 5)

The following example describes a function call. You will be using *the moveForward(piece: steps:)* function to move the rook 5 forward by five steps.

In the following example, rook is defined as a variable.

Functions in Swift has two sections:

1. Function definition.
2. Calling function.

A function is defined before it is called. In other words, you have to prepare a task before you can perform it. A function can be called numerous times.

Assume that your chess game has various functions such as *setupBoard(), vaidateMove()* and *isCheckmate()*. Rather than writing each scenario inside the chess game manually, you need to include abstractions several times to perform the common tasks such as validating a chess move or confirming a player has checkmate.

```
func moveForward(piece: String, steps: Int)
{
    print("Moving the \(piece) piece \(steps) steps forward...")
}
moveForward(piece: "Queen", steps: 3)
```

This is what happens:

1. A function defined by *func moveForward (piece: String....* Beginning on the first line.

2. This function referred to as *moveForward (piece: "Queen," steps: 3)* on the last line.

Let's look at the function definition first. Here's how it operates:

- Func describes the keyword that you apply to begin a function declaration.

- The name of the function is called moveForward.

- (piece: string, steps:Int) describe the function parameters.

- *The piece* describes the first parameter name, and String is the type.

- *Steps* describe the function's second parameter name, and Int refers to the type.

➢ Between the {} brackets go the body of the function.

The most critical parts include the function name, the parameters, and the function body. The name of the function defines the task that the function can do, and its parameters define the type of input the function requires.

The body of the function features the code of the function. This is the code that gets executed when the function is called.

Let's return to the function call. In the last line of the previous example, the call of the function has this line:

```
moveForward(piece: "Queen", steps: 3
```

You have to create arguments for the function. For example, "queen" and 3. This is the initial input of the function.

A function call will accurately execute the code inside the function body. The best thing about functions is that you can call them numerous times, while the function is defined only once. For instance:

```
moveForward(piece: "Queen", steps: 3)
moveForward(piece: "Rook", steps: 5)
moveForward(piece: "Pawn", steps: 1)
```

Within the function, you can write the code to execute all the moves for several parts. Instead of writing the code for each manually, you can create an abstraction that can do the multiple moves. Do you see the way abstraction is a great principle?

Function arguments and parameters

A function can hold zero, one or even more parameters. A parameter is an input for a function. Here's an example:

```swift
func greeting(user: String)
{
    print("Hello, \(user). How are you?")
}
greeting(user: "Arthur")
```

In this code, the parameter of the function is *user*, i.e. *greeting (user:)*. The parameter is commonly applied as the input for the function. Therefore, the function can "greet" the user.

The function parameter is written after the function name, and it is wrapped in parentheses. Multiple function parameters are distinguished by commas. Examples include:

```swift
func setupBoard()
func greeting(user: String)
func compare(a: String, b: String)
```

When you call a function in Swift, you need to write the name of the parameter, unless it is further specified, for instance:

greeting(user: "Arthur")

In this example, "Arthur" is an argument. This is often confusing to many new developers. They find it difficult to differentiate between a parameter and an argument.

- If you are going to define a function, you will have to define parameters. Inside the body of the function, you can include parameters as the local variables.

- If you are going to call a function, you will have to use arguments to call the function. This is a value that is allocated to a parameter.

You can memorize the following mnemonic:

"A parameter is the 'parking spot'. An argument is the "car" you park in the 'parking spot'.

In IOS development, you will always refer to it as the parameter.

Another thing that you need to understand are the argument labels and parameter names.

```
func authenticateUser(withUsername username:String, andPassword password: String)
{
    print("Authenticating \(username) with password ***")
}
authenticateUser(withUsername: "Zaphod", andPassword: "h3art0fg0ld")
```

The parameters and arguments for the following function have *withUsername* and *username*, and "andpassword" and *password*. You can also identify *withUsername* and *andPassword* within the function call located in the last line. So what is that?

Well, *withUsername* is the argument label, and *username* is the parameter name. When a parameter contains an argument label, you will see the argument rather than the parameter name when you call the function.

It is important to note the difference because when you apply *argument labels,* it's going to be common in practical IOS development. Most of the Cocoa Touch SDKs contain argument labels to ensure that functions become descriptive.

You will require the argument label when you call the function. It is an additional description of the function's argument. Inside the function, you only need to apply the shorter parameter name.

The Function Return Types and Values

The same way functions contain input; they also have output. It is logical that functions should have output.

Functions in Swift that have return type apply the following syntax.

```swift
func abs(_ a: Int) -> Int
{
    if a < 0 {
        return a * -1
    }
    
    return a
}

let result = abs(-11)
print(result)
```

In this example, the ->Int will define the return type. You have to show that the above function will return a value of Int. The -> is a "single arrow".

Within the function, a value is returned using the "return" keyword. This will prevent the execution of the function at that point, and display a return value of the expression.

In the above example:

- …a * -1 is returned whenever a is smaller than zero.

- …and if not, a is returned.

For the abs() function, this effectively returns the absolute value of a. The function will often return a positive integer.

For Swift, the output of the function is delivered to any function call. As you can see in the above example, the value abs(-11) is allocated to the constant result. For example:

Let result = abs(-11)

It is also possible to output a single function as input for the next. For example:

Print(abs(-11))

The function can also be included in expressions. For example:

Let result = abs(11) + abs(-11)

Functions are like "first-class citizens" in Swift language, what this means is that you can call them from any place, the same way you do for the variable. You can build expressions using functions, the same way you build expressions using literals and variables.

Below is another great example:

```swift
func fibonacci(_ i: Int) -> Int {
    if i <= 2 {
        return 1
    } else {
        return fibonacci(i - 1) + fibonacci(i - 2)
    }
}

for i in 1...10 {
    print(fibonacci(i))
}
```

This function uses recursion to compute the nth value in the Fibonacci series.

Generics in Swift Explained

Generics is a great feature applied in the Swift language. At first, it can be a bit puzzling. In this section, we shall look at the way generics operate, and how you can use them.

As you know, Swift has a "strong type system." Once the variable is declared as an integer, you can't just move straight and assign it a string value. For example:

```
var text:String = "Hello world!"
text = 5
// Output: error: cannot assign value of type 'Int' to type 'String'
```

Once you declare it a string, it will remain a string. It is not possible to allocate it a value of type Int to a string variable type.

This level of strictness is a great thing because it assists a person making programming mistakes. Well, suppose you need to work with the data types that are not that strict?

Here's an example. Let's assume you have created a **Generics in Swift Explained**

Generics is a great feature in Swift programming language. At first, it can be a bit confusing. In this section, we shall look at the way generics operate, and how you can use them.

As you know, Swift has a strong type system. Once the variable is declared as a string, you can't just move straight and assign it an integer value. For example:

```
var text:String = "Hello world!"
text = 5
// Output: error: cannot assign value of type 'Int' to type 'String'
```

Once you declare it a string, it will remain a string. It is not possible to allocate it a value of type Int to a string variable type.

This level of strictness is a great thing because it assists a person in making programming mistakes. Well, suppose you need to work with the data types that are not that strict?

Here's an example. Let's assume you have created a simple function that will add a single number to another. For instance:

```
func addition(a: Int, b: Int) -> Int
{
    return a + b
}

let result = addition(a: 42, b: 99)
print(result)
// Output: 141
```

The function accepts two kinds of parameters, i.e. a and b of type int, and it will return a value of type Int. The + operator will add numbers and return the result.

Now let's say you want to expand the function so that you can include other types, for example, the Double and Float. It cannot be a function if it cannot add decimal point numbers.

Thus, you write a new function.

```
func addition(a: Double, b: Double) -> Double
{
    return a + b
}
```

Now you have repeated the code. This is not a good thing going by the principle of coding.

Let's use Generic Functions and Placeholders
When you apply generics, you can basically write clear, reusable and flexible code. Thus, you will avoid writing the same type of code twice, and this will allow you to create generic code.

Here's an example, we have taken the original addition(a:b) function, and turned it into a generic function. For example:

```
func addition<T: Numeric>(a: T, b: T) -> T
{
    return a + b
}
```

Modest function that will add a single number to another. For instance:

```
func addition(a: Int, b: Int) -> Int
{
    return a + b
}

let result = addition(a: 42, b: 99)
print(result)
// Output: 141
```

The function accepts two kinds of parameters, i.e. a and b of type int, and it will return a value of type Int. The + operator will add numbers and return the result.

Now let's say you want to expand the function so that you can include other types, for example, the Double and Float. It cannot be a function if it cannot add decimal point numbers.

Thus, you write a new function.

```
func addition(a: Double, b: Double) -> Double
{
    return a + b
}
```

Now you have repeated the code. This is not a good thing going by the principle of coding.

Let's use Generic Functions and Placeholders

When you apply generics, you can basically write clear, reusable and flexible code. Thus, you will avoid writing the same type of code twice, and this will allow you to create generic code.

Here's an example, we have taken the original addition(a:b) function, and turned it into a generic function. For example:

```swift
func addition<T: Numeric>(a: T, b: T) -> T
{
    return a + b
}
```

For Loop

In programming, for loops are very important. With for loop, it is possible to repeat code and improve the working of your code. For the Swift language, you can use the repeat-while, while and for-in loop.

This part will teach you the way you can use the for-in loop, and how you can also use while and repeat-while.

In the Swift language, the for loop is very useful to any developer.

The for loop in Swift

Swift language has a simple structure for the for a loop. Here's the structure:

```swift
for item in items {
// Do this }
```

In Swift language, the for loop must feature a *for* and *in* keywords. The loop will later accept the sequence if items, and loop over the items. In the above structure, each item exists as a variable within the loop. The repeated code within the body of the loop can be described to means this way, for each "item" found in "items," you need to implement this code.

In most of the programming languages, the for loop is inferred as the for-each. A typical structure of the for loop will have a syntax as shown below:

```
for(i = 0; i < n; i++) { ... }
```

But the Swift language is unique because the *for-in* syntax can iterate different ranges of numbers, even when both the strings, and collections, have the same format.

Object types like dictionaries, arrays, ranges, and strings are describing as sequences. Sequences will provide support to the for-loop.

Here's an example:

```
for n in 1...5 {
    print(n)
}
// Output: 1 2 3 4 5
```

This example features a "closed range operator". The operator defines a range that starts from 1-5. For this reason, you can repeat the above instruction, a limited number of occasions.

How to loop over a collection of items using For-in

You understand that arrays and dictionaries feature various types of collections. It is possible to define your collections from the "Realm database" framework.

Here's an example:

```
let names = ["Arthur", "Zaphod", "Trillian", "Ford", "Marvin"]
for name in names {
    print(name)
}
```

This code shown above will display strings inside the array one by one. The names of the variable don't have any explicit type, but it's considered an array. Therefore, the variable type of *name* has to include a String.

Below is an example:

```
let numbers = [1, 2, 3, 4, 5, 6]
var sum = 0

for i in numbers {
    sum += i
}

print(sum)
```

If you want to develop a function that will return the total of an array of integers. Then the code that you must use is shown below:

```
func sum(_ numbers:[Int]) -> Int
{
    var sum = 0

    for n in numbers {
        sum += n
    }

    return sum
}

let result = sum([23, 11, 9, 3, 24, 77])
print(result) // Output: 147
```

Also, you can include subscript syntax and the index numbers while working with a set. The for loops are useful especially when you need to implement the same style for various UI elements such as buttons.

For example:

```
let buttons = [loginButton, signupButton, facebookButton]

for button in buttons {
    button.backgroundColor = UIColor.red
    button.layer.cornerRadius = 5.0
}
```

To loop over a data collection, in a line graph. You may need to draw the graph by iterating every data point with the help of a for a loop.

```
let points = [0.1, 0.2, 0.3, 0.5, 0.7, 0.8]

for x in 0..<points.count {
    let y = points[x]
    graph.drawPoint(x, y)
}
```

If you want to send an alert the followers of each user, for example in the social network app, you will need to apply the for loop like this:

```
for uid in user.followers {
    sendNotification(withUID: uid)
}
```

How to loop over ranges using for-in

Now that you have just looked at ranges for some time let's go deeper. It is easy to assume that you are applying the for loop to go over collections, but when you can iterate ranges, it becomes even fascinating.

This code contains a closed range operator:

```
for n in 1...5 {
    print(n)
}
```

The closed range operator.... Will define a struct of *ClosedRange* type. This closed range accepts two parameters: the lower bound and the upper bound. It will then generate a range between the numbers; this includes the last one.

You can also develop ranges by applying the text characters. For example:

```
let xyz = "x"..."z"
print(xyz.contains("y"))
// Output: true
```

The *ClosedRange* struct is related with the *Range,* using the half-open range operator. This will create a range between the upper and the lower bound.

For example:

```
for i in 0..<5 {
    print(i)
}
// Output: 0 1 2 3 4
```

You will realize that the half-open range type of operator will be important in programming because you will be handling ranges that start from 0 to for example the end of an array.

The index located in the last item of the array will always be equivalent to the size of the array minus one. If you would like a range that begins from 0 to the end of the array, you perhaps find the following:

```
for i in 0..<items.count {
    // Do stuff...
}
```

Note

Closed ranges cannot be empty, and the reason is that they will always feature a "distance" between the lower and upper bound-even when it's 0. On the other hand, half-open ranges can still be empty because the upper section cannot be included inside the range.

Looping using while and repeat-while

To loop over a set of instructions is a great thing in programming because:

- Computation and automation have nothing else besides repetition of a collection of instructions. If you are realizing that you are implementing a specific part of code many times using the same outcomes, then you may have to think twice whether to apply a loop.

- The Don't Repeat-Yourself principle – as it states, you aren't supposed to repeat anything. This also applied for loops. In other words, if you are doing a task four times, when you can do it once and repeat it four times. It's better to use a loop.

The for-in loop is not the only kind of syntax that Swift depends on. There are others:

- The *while* loop will repeat the code until the time it is false. It is important when you want to repeat a given task, but you don't know the number of times. This state is determined at the beginning of a loop. For example:

```
while(condition == true) {
    // Repeat this
}
```

- The *repeat-while* loops are similar to while loop, but the difference is that it determines a condition at the end of the loop. In this case, it will always run once:

```
repeat {
    // Do this
} while(condition == true)
```

The while, for-in and repeat-while statements are basic strategies used to repeat code. When it comes to Swift, you will come across different concepts of iteration. It is important to look at other options if not, you can easily write inefficient and extensive code.

Some examples:

- If you want to change arrays, for example, you have a function that you want to apply for every array element or restrict the array to a single result, then you should go for the filter (), reduce (), map () high-order functions.

- If you want to display cells in a table view, you need to apply the default UITableView to load the cell, output and reuse it. While this doesn't require a loop, it will repeat a collection of instructions numerous times.

- When you want to write a particular function that accepts its output as input for various iteration, you need to apply recursion rather than a loop.

Chapter 5

Map, Reduce and Filter in Swift

The Swift Functions Map, Filter and Reduce can be very challenging to understand. This is very true if you have always written for-loops to create a solution for iteration problems.

The Map, Reduce, and Filter functions may originate from the real of functional programming. In Swift language, you can apply Map, Reduce and Filter to loop over types of collection such as Dictionary and Array without application for-loop.

When creating apps, you basically apply the procedural or object-oriented style. Functional programming is different because it focuses on functions. No "states,," no variables, no for –loops-just functions.

The Swift language is best for functional programming. There is no need to write functional code, but you only have to include concepts from functional programming such as Map, Reduce, and Filter.

Filter, Reduce, and Map is usually referred to as "higher-order functions," because the "functions accept functions as input" and will return functions as output.

Swift will return results of operation when you apply a higher-order function, while "pure" functional language will return a set of functions.

In case you're saying: "I don't need functional programming, because my apps don't do that! -don't stop here.

Map, Reduce, and Filter has been used in numerous instances:

- Filtering cost, to meet a specific threshold, before you include a line graph.

- Mapping several operations on hashtags.

- Limiting thousands of movie rating into an average rating.

You may perhaps have fixed all these problems by applying a for-loop, but you will realize that map, reduce, and filter functions bring more readable, concise and performant code.

In the following guide, you'll learn how to apply a Map, Reduce, and Filter functions. You'll implement the following functions on collection types, such as Array.

Below is an overview
- The *map* function will loop over each item in a collection, and involves an operation to every element in the collection.

- The *reduce* function will loop over each item inside a collection, and combine it into a single value.

- The *filter* function loops every item found in the collection, and outputs a collection that has only items that meet a specified condition.

Put differently
- The *map* function will include a function for each item in the collection. Look at "mapping" one set of values into a separate set of values.

- The "reduce" function turns a collection into a single value. You can think of it as reducing numerous values into a single one.

- The filter function basically outputs an array of values that when passed an if-statement condition, and only when the condition results in true.

Fun fact

The *MapReduce* is important in Big Data processing concept, where the intensive operation is included in parallel to the collection. An example may include creating a one-page summary of a book into one, and then storing the words in alphabetical boxes.

Applying the Map Function

The *map* function will loop over each item in a collection and implements an operation to every element in the collection. This will return an array of items, which the operation executed.

Here's an example:

Let's assume that you have an array of temperatures in Celcius that you would like to change to Fahrenheit.

You may apply a for-loop:

```
let celcius = [-5.0, 10.0, 21.0, 33.0, 50.0]
var fahrenheit:[Double] = []

for value in celcius {
    fahrenheit += [value * (9/5) + 32]
}

print(fahrenheit)
// Output: [23.0, 50.0, 69.8, 91.4, 122.0]
```

Though this code operates fine, it's not the most effective. You require a mutable "helper" variable *Fahrenheit* to retain the computed conversions as you work through them, and you require three lines of code for the conversion itself.

Examine the code sample below, by applying the *map* function.

```
let celcius = [-5.0, 10.0, 21.0, 33.0, 50.0]
let fahrenheit = celcius.map { $0 * (9/5) + 32 }
print(fahrenheit)
// Output: [23.0, 50.0, 69.8, 91.4, 122.0]
```

What takes place here?

- First, a constant *celsius* is determined; this constant is of Array Double, and initialized with several random Celcius values.

- Secondly, the function *map* is referred on the constant celsius. The function contains a single argument, a closure, the closure converts from Celcius to Fahrenheit.

- Lastly, the result is printed out.

Let's examine the closure. If you have used closure before, you will notice the "short-hand closure syntax." This is a short cut way to program a closure, and it leaves out most of the syntax of the closure.

You typically work with input, for example, $0, and squiggly brackets. The $0 is the first input parameter for the closure. In case the closure contains numerous parameters, the second parameter may be $1, the third $2, etc.

Below is the "expanded" code:

```
let celcius = [-5.0, 10.0, 21.0, 33.0, 50.0]

let fahrenheit = celcius.map({ (value: Double) -> Double in
    return value * (9/5) + 32
})
print(fahrenheit)
```

The initial map function call, and the closure look as follows:

```
... = celcius.map({ (value: Double) -> Double in
      return value * (9/5) + 32
})
```

Notice the map function is applied on the array *celcius*. The following map function will accept one argument: the closure.

The first part of the closure, beginning with {, describes the closure has a single parameter value of type Double, and has to return a Double type of value. The closure body beginning with return, does return the result of the Celsius to Fahrenheit conversion.

When you compare the short-hand closure syntax to the code expanded above, you'll notice that:

- The function parentheses (and) are excluded because you can omit them when the last parameter of a function call contains a closure.

- The () -> in part can be excluded because Swift infer that you are applying a Double parameter as the input, and it is expected to return a Double. Since you have the *value variable left,* you can apply the short-hand $0.

- The return statement can be excluded too because the closure is required to return a result of an expression.

Although the code above has *Double* types, you aren't limited to the following types. The final type of a *map* function can contain different type than what you place into it, and you can apply map on the Dictionary too.

Using the Reduce Function

The *reduce* function will loop over each item in a collection and combines them into a single value. Consider it as literally cutting down multiple values to a single value.

The Reduce function is basically the most difficult of Map, Reduce, and Filter to understand. How can you move from one collection of values to the next?

Some examples:

- Building a sum of multiple values
- Concatenating set of strings

Conclusion

The Swift language is a great way to write software, regardless of whether it's servers, desktops, phones and or anything that runs a code. The language is fast, secure and interactive. It integrates the best in interactive programming with wisdom from the expansive Apple engineering culture and the extensive contributions from the open-source community. The compiler is designed for performance, and the language is improved for development, without affecting each other.

Swift is a friendly language to newbies. It is expressive and enjoyable like scripting languages. As simple, expressive, and clean Swift is, its simple grammar and syntax make it easy to read and write. The fact that it is concise, it shortens the development time.

Safety is another idea behind the launch of Swift to IOS developers. It is perhaps prone to fewer errors, because of its error handling abilities, and improved typing technology. Therefore, the language has fewer crashes than Objective-C.

Even with the many advantages that the language boasts, nothing is perfect. There are a few problems that developers experience when they use the language. There is no question that the language has been rapidly changing. But we cannot ignore that it is still a young language, in particular when you compare it to Objective-C. This is the reason why you will experience some problems when you use this language.